1000
Artists' Books

QUARRY

First published in the United States of America in 2012 by
Quarry Books, a member of
Quayside Publishing Group
100 Cummings Center
Suite 406-L
Beverly, Massachusetts 01915-6101
Telephone: (978) 282-9590
Fax: (978) 283-2742
www.quarrybooks.com
Visit www.Craftside.Typepad.com for a behind-the-scenes peek at our crafty world!

10 9 8 7 6 5 4 3 2 1

ISBN: 978-1-59253-774-7

Digital edition published in 2012
eISBN: 978-1-61059-947-4

Library of Congress Cataloging-in-Publication Data available

Design: Sandra Salamony
Cover Images: tk from designer

Works by Richard Minsky appeared previously in *The Book Art of Richard Minsky*
published by George Braziller, Inc, © 2011 Richard Minsky.

Printed in China

1000 Artists' Books

EXPLORING
the
BOOK
as ART

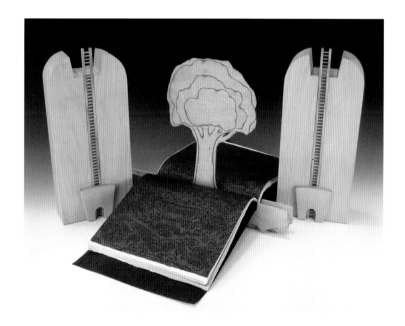

SANDRA SALAMONY *with* PETER & DONNA THOMAS

Quarry Books
100 Cummings Center, Suite 406L
Beverly, MA 01915

quarrybooks.com • craftside.typepad.com

CONTENTS

Introduction

WHAT IS AN ARTISTS' BOOK? This question does not have a simple answer. Even if it were only, "What is a book?" the question would not be any easier to answer. This is because the word "book" is regularly used to imply both the content and the object itself. It is not unusual for a person to say, "I wrote a book," and by that mean they wrote something to be printed in a book, rather than actually writing the words of a story in a book. And likewise it is not unusual for a person to say, "I made a book," when they have bound a blank book that has no words or images inside. The concept of 'bookness' is not as simple as it may seem.

When the word "artist" is added to the word "book," the result becomes even more complex. What is art? The question has been argued, discussed and dissected for centuries. As with book, the definition of art changes and often depends on whether the process or the product is being considered. For example, cooking can be an art, but the meal created might not be a work of art.

It was not until the mid-1980s that the term "artists' books" crept into common usage as a way to describe books made by artists. Before that the term was more commonly used to describe the *livre d'artiste,* books created by a publisher to pair illustrations by famous artists with well-known texts. In the same way that the first cars were called "horseless carriages," the phrase "artists' books" described both medium and product in terms of objects that already existed. There may be a better name, but so far there is no agreement on what it might be. But there is agreement to use an apostrophe and place it after the "s," claiming

the phrase to describe the genre of art works made by book artists.

In 2010 and 2011, Donna and I traveled around the country in our gypsy wagon artists' bookmobile (20,000 miles, 35 states), teaching classes and talking about the book arts. Between stops, people would often chase us down to look inside the gypsy wagon and find out what we were doing. When we told them we were book artists, they would often get a confused look, so we would explain: "A book artist is a person who makes books as their form of artistic expression, and an artists' book is the creation of a book artist. A book artist makes books like a painter makes paintings." Though simplistic, this answer often helped them understand that an artists' book is a work of art and not simply a means of conveying information.

I often used the gypsy wagon as a metaphor for the artist's book, saying, "when a person looks inside a regular RV what do they think? Usually nothing special, or something like, 'How practical.' But when people see our gypsy wagon they get excited, curious, and something magical happens. Commercially produced books are like regular RVs: practical and full of information. Artists' books are like our gypsy wagon: they inspire imagination and wonder and share something of the artist who created them."

How does one know if a work of art is an artists' book or only a 3-D painting or a sculpture? What are the physical and conceptual attributes that define an artists' book? Generally, if an object has book-like qualities recognizable by either the maker or the viewer, then it is fair to call it an artists' book. Some people get

Ruscha's "Twentysix Gasoline Stations" (1963) is one of the earliest examples of a modern book conceived as an art work. ©ED RUSCHA. COURTESY GAGOSIAN GALLERY

caught up trying to decide if a work of art is, or is not, an artists' book. I find it more interesting to discover what the book-like qualities are by asking questions such as: "Where on the scale of object to information does it fit?"

An artists' book with pages that can be turned is a sequential art form that goes beyond the ordinary three dimensions of other sculptural art works. A masterpiece of the artists' book can be enjoyed as a two-dimensional object when viewed in a photograph, as a three-dimensional object when on display in a glass case, and as a four dimensional object when held and read. If you find yourself frustrated because you cannot read the text or see the sequence when viewing the images in this book, try enjoying the two dimensional experience. If you really want to read or hold the book, you can always contact the artist to buy a copy or visit a library or museum to see it.

Most art forms have recognized genres. Paintings can be labeled as landscape, abstract, or portrait. A film can be called a noir, comedy, or drama. Artists' books do not yet have commonly recognized genres. To organize the 1,000 images for this book, I decided to focus solely on the structure, and defined four structural "genres": codex books (books with pages joined to make a spine), accordion and foldable books (books with multiple-fold pages), single-sheet books (books with single-sheet pages), and sculptural books (books made from objects and objects made into books). Detailed descriptions of these genres are given at the beginning of each chapter.

While traveling around the country, we were frequently asked if we worried about com-puters and e-books taking the place of physical books and running us out of a job. I'm not worried. This is an exciting time to be involved in the book arts. Since the invention of the printing press, the book as a medium for the artist has been encumbered by function. Today, in the same way that photography set painting free, the personal computer has released the book from its servitude to information. Freed from function, the book can be an aesthetic object, a work of art. When electronic books become the primary distribution source for the written word, people will turn to physical books for aesthetic satisfaction.

The book, with so many possible forms of expression, is clearly the most complex and versatile art medium that exists. I believe that very soon artists will discover how to exploit these potentials to create works of art that today are still unimaginable. It seems very likely that by the end of the twenty-first century, paintings and sculptures will be gathering dust in museum storage rooms while the galleries will be full of artists' books. Perhaps some of those art works will be books you first saw pictured here in this edition of *1,000 Artists' Books*.

—*Peter Thomas*
Peter and Donna Thomas,
Santa Cruz, California

Hedi Kyle's first "flag book," April's Diary 1979, was a ground-breaking structural exploration.

Rebis Press's 1981 "Hats Off" pushed the limits of the fine press aesthetic with its nontraditional binding materials and unusual structure.
JOHN WEHRLE

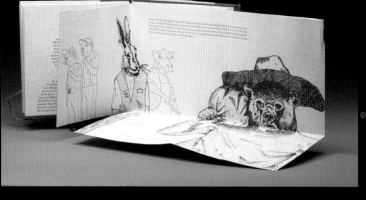

Chapter 1:

CODEX BOOKS

*books with pages joined
to make a spine*

Books made with single-fold pages,
joined to make a spine:

- pamphlets, case bindings, designer
bindings, long stitch bindings, coptic
stitch bindings, stab bindings, French
door bindings

Books made with single sheet pages,
joined to make a spine:

- perfect bindings, drum bindings,
flip books, stapled pamphlets,
post and screw

0001—
0354

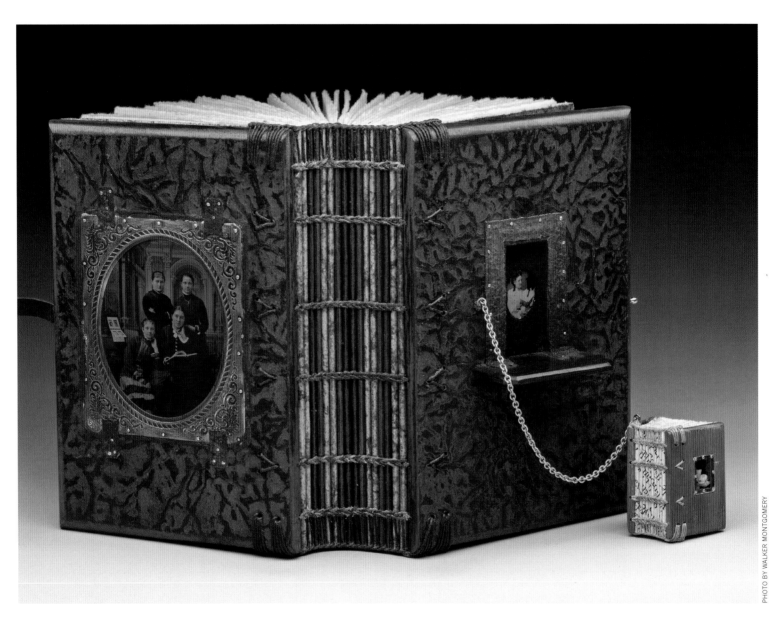

0001

Daniel Essig, USA

0002, 0003, 0004
Daniel Essig, USA

PHOTO BY SIBILA SAVAGE

PHOTO BY SIBILA SAVAGE

0005, 0006
Alisa Golden, never mind the press, USA

0007, 0008
Paul Henry, UK

0009, 0010
Cynthia Colbert, USA

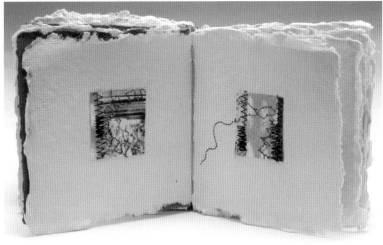

0011, 0012
Bessie Smith Moulton, USA

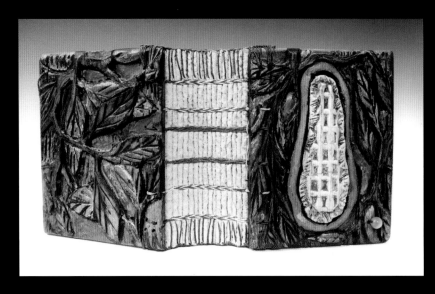

0013

Nancy Jean Wallace, Too Many Shoes Studio, USA

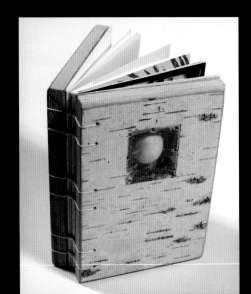

0016, 0017, 0018
Paul Henry, UK

0019
Barbara Simler, CANADA

0020, 0021
Genie Shenk, USA

0022, 0023
Bertha Rogers, Six Swans Artist Editions, USA

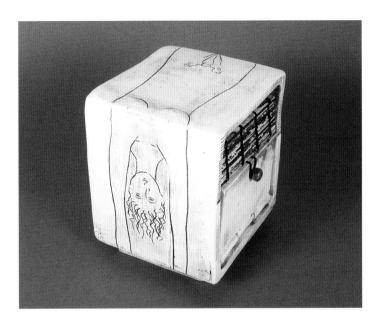

0024, 0025, 0026
Judith Serebrin, Judith of Serebrin
Books & Prints, USA

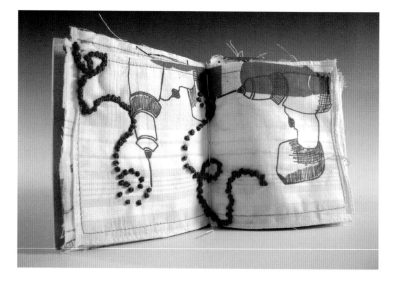

0027, 0028, 0029
Erin Sweeney, Lovely In The Home Press, USA

0030, 0031
Judith Hoffman, USA

0032, 0033
Hanne Niederhausen, USA

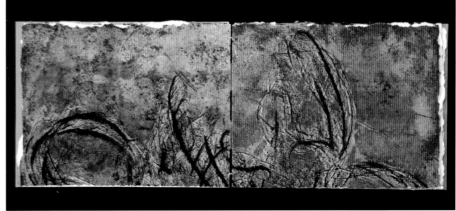

0034, 0035, 0036
Caren Heft, Arcadian Press, USA

0037, 0038
Robyn Hunt, Robin Sparrow Books, NEW ZEALAND

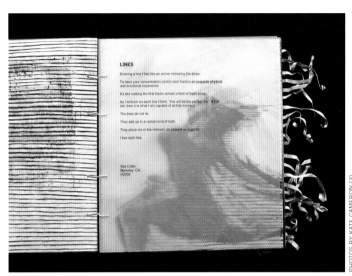

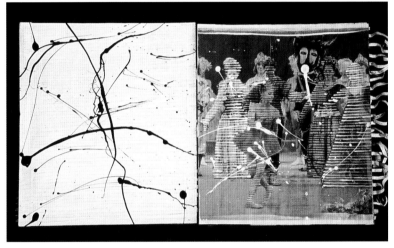

[0039, 0040, 0041
Sas Colby, USA

[0042, 0043
Genie Shenk, USA

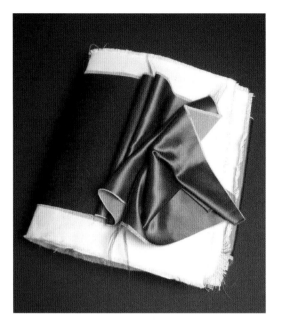 

0044, 0045
Stephanie Sherwood, USA

0046
e Bond, roughdrAft books, USA

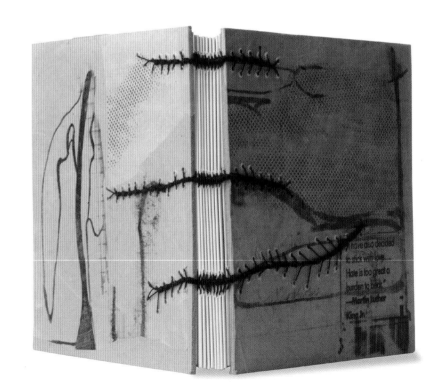

[0047, 0048
Dee Collins, USA

[0049, 0050, 0051
Michelle Wilson, Rocinante Press, USA

0052, 0053
Ellen Knudson, Crooked Letter Press, USA

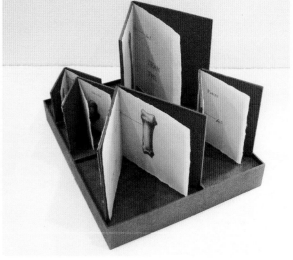

0054, 0055
Stefan Volatile-Wood, USA

0056, 0057
Beata Wehr, USA

0058, 0059
**Purgatory Pie Press, Dikko Faust + Esther K Smith,
collaborating artist: Susan Happersett,** USA

PHOTO BY BETH FORMAN

0060, 0061, 0062
Lisa Rappoport,
Littoral Press, USA

0063
Peter & Donna Thomas, USA

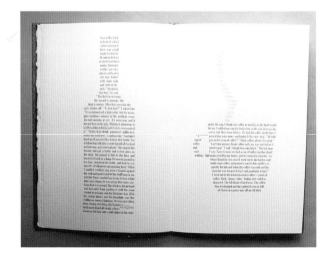

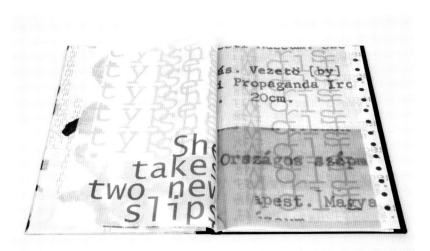

0064, 0065, 0066
Robbin Ami Silverberg,
Dobbin Mill/Dobbin Books, USA

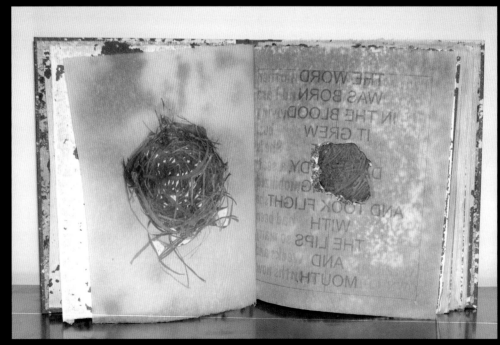

0067, 0068, 0069

Robbin Ami Silverberg, Dobbin Mill/Dobbin Books, USA

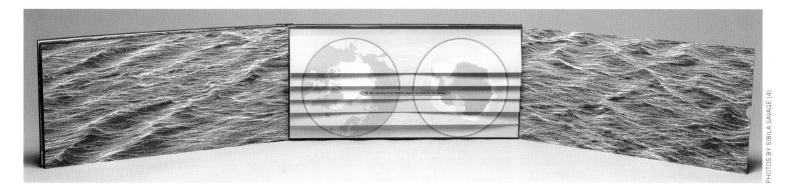

0070, 0071, 0072, 0073
Julie Chen, Flying Fish Press, USA

0074, 0075
Peter Madden, USA

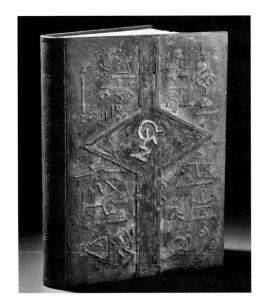

0076, 0077
Timothy C. Ely, USA

0078, 0079, 0080
Peter & Donna Thomas, USA

0081
Mary McCarthy and Shirley Veenema, USA

0082, 0083
Rocco Scary, USA

0084, 0085
Velma Bolyard, Wake Robin Papers, USA

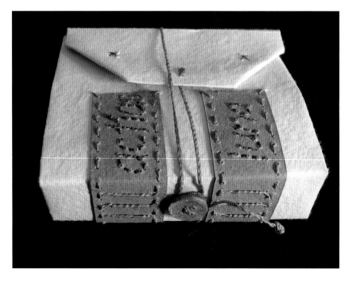

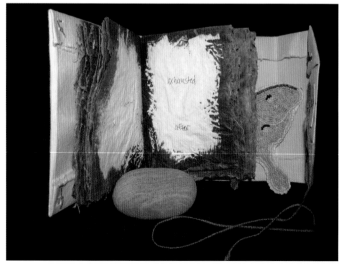

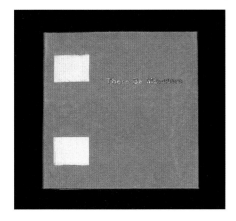

0086, 0087, 0088

Chad Pastotnik,
Deep Wood Press, USA

0089, 0090

Aimee Lee, USA

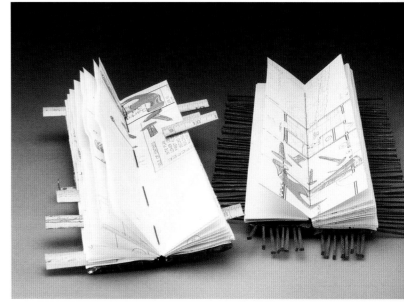

0091, 0092
Erin Sweeney, Lovely In The Home Press, USA

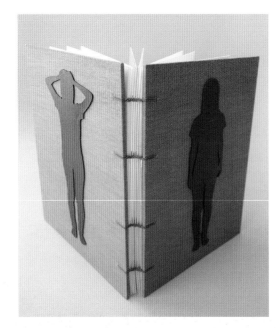
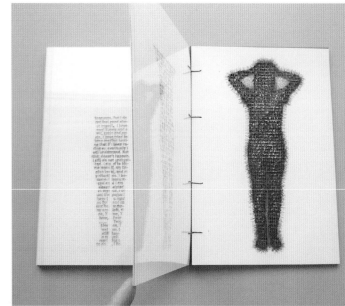

0093, 0094
Jana Sim, USA

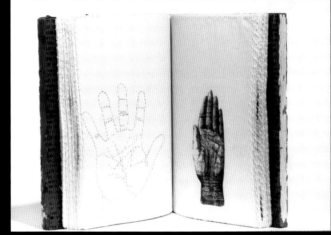

0095, 0096, 0097
Peter Madden, USA

0098
Jeanne Bennett, USA

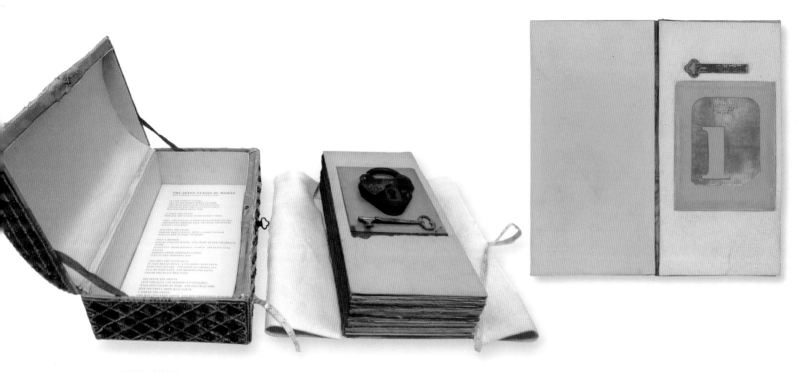

[0099, 0100
Dorothy Simpson Krause, Viewpoint Editions, USA

[0101, 0102
Deborah Kogan, USA

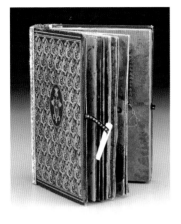

PHOTOS BY JOHN POLAK PHOTOGRAPHY (3)

0103, 0104, 0105
Sharon McCartney, USA

0106, 0107
Maureen Piggins, CANADA

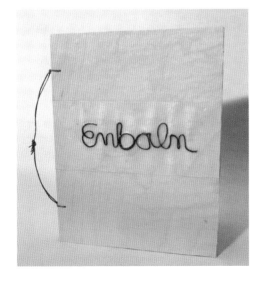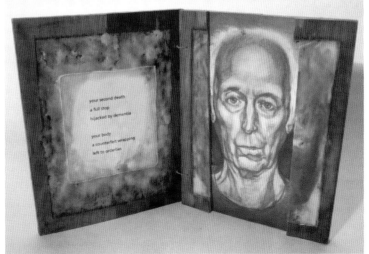

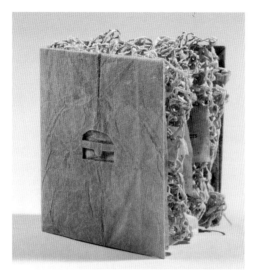

They floated in the wind
Mixed with wild ginger, with onions
Got buried in dead leaves
Rotted with the oranges
But paper rescued them
Grabbed hold and held

Breath became stone hard
Words turned armies to monsters
Dreams into nightmares

Was pap...
Before p...

PHOTOS BY STEFAN HAGEN (2)

0108, 0109
Aimee Lee, USA

In case of panic
by Kelly O'Brien

PHOTOS BY JIM VECCHIONE (2)

0110, 0111
Kelly O'Brien, TurningPointe Press, GERMANY

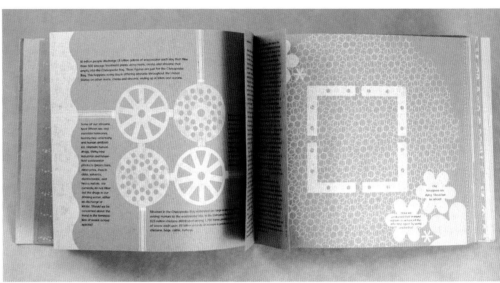

0112, 0113, 0114

Elsi Vassdal Ellis, EVE Press,
USA

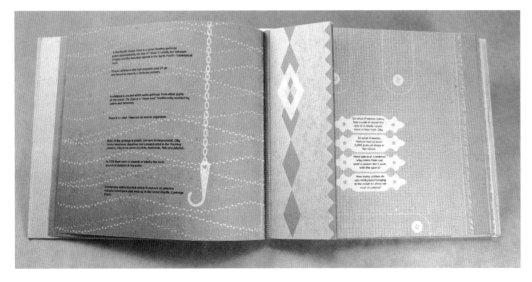

0115, 0116
Buzz Spector, USA

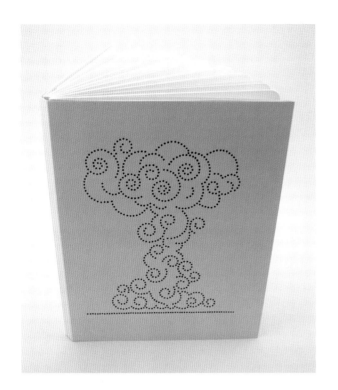

0117, 0118, 0119
Elsi Vassdal Ellis, EVE Press,
USA

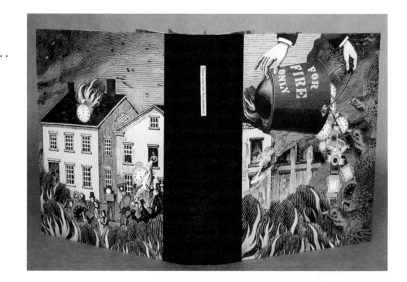

0120
Heather Crossley, AUSTRALIA

0121, 0122, 0123
Elsi Vassdal Ellis, EVE Press,
USA

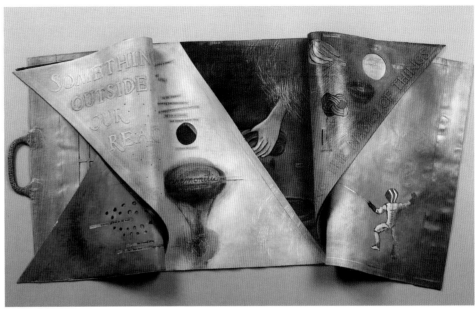

0124, 0125
Sas Colby, USA

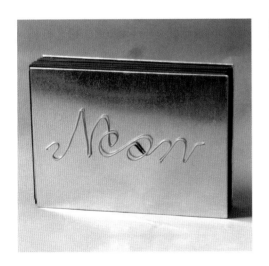

0126, 0127
Thomas Parker Williams, USA

0128, 0129

Guylaine Couture, CANADA

0130
Margaret Beech, Calligrapher & Bookartist, UK

0131, 0132
Patricia Sarrafian Ward, USA

0133, 0134
Alisa Golden, never mind the press, USA

0135, 0136
Eileen Arnow-Levine, USA

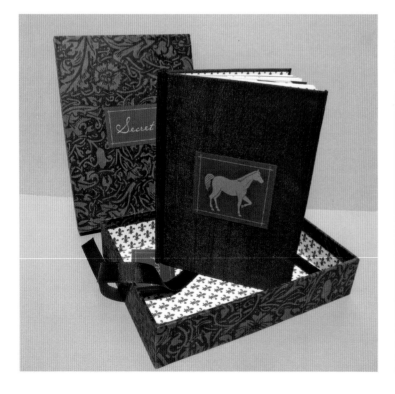

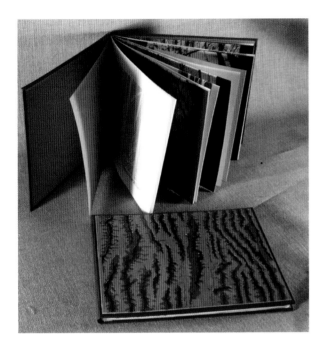

0137, 0138
Thomas Parker Williams, USA

0139, 0140
Miyako Akai, Kototsubo, JAPAN

0141, 0142, 0143
Melissa Jay Craig, USA

0144, 0145
Susan Kapuscinski Gaylord, USA

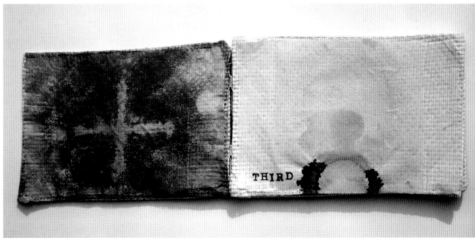

THIRD

0146, 0147
Lucy Baxandall, UK

[0148, 0149
Karen Kunc, Blue Heron Press, USA

[0150, 0151
Michael Andrews,
Bombshelter Press, USA

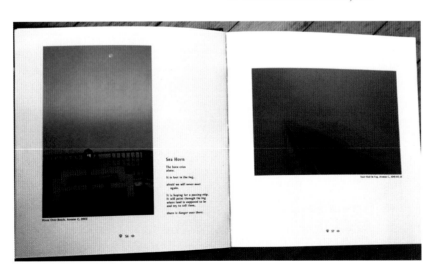

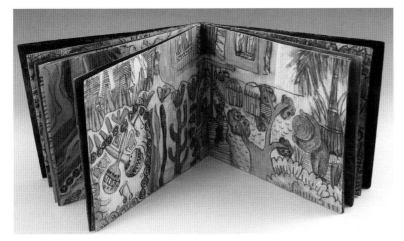

[0152, 0153, 0154
Jill K. Berry, USA

[0155, 0156
Jeffrey Morin, sailorBOYpress, USA

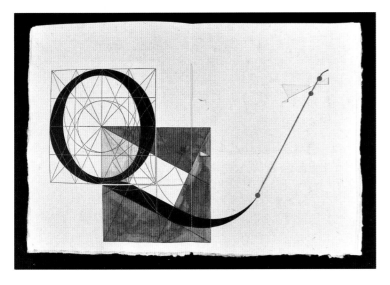

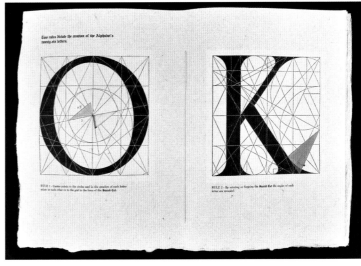

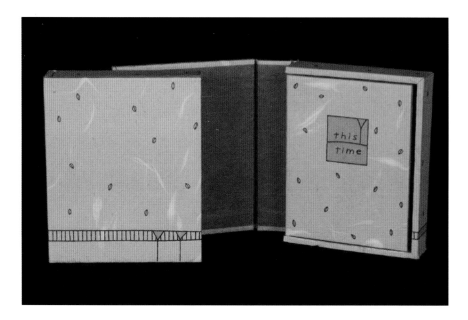

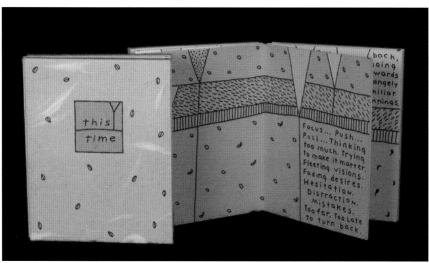

0157, 0158
Jody Williams, Flying Paper Press, USA

0159, 0160
C J. Shane, USA

0161, 0162
Lisa Cheney-Jorgensen, RightSide Design, USA

0163
Dayle Doroshow, Zingaro, USA

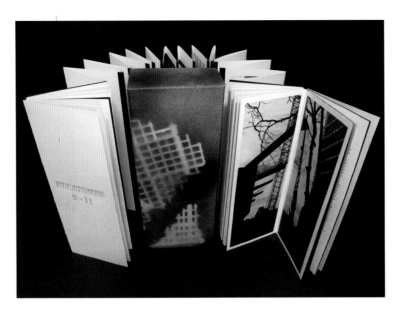

0164, 0165
Maria G. Pisano, Memory Press, USA

0166, 0167, 0168
Alicia Bailey, USA

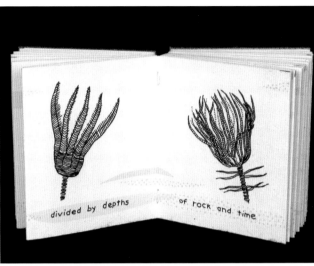

0169, 0170
Jody Williams, Flying Paper Press, USA

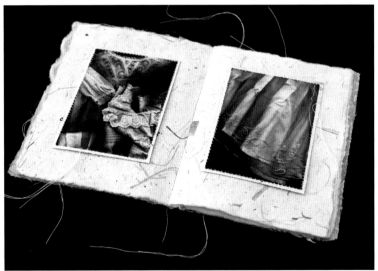

0171, 0172
Jeanne Germani, CANADA

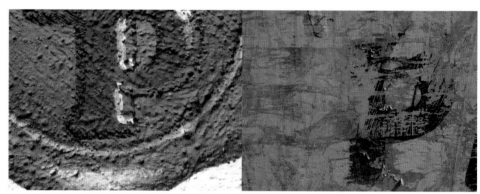

0173, 0174, 0175
Joan Lyons, USA

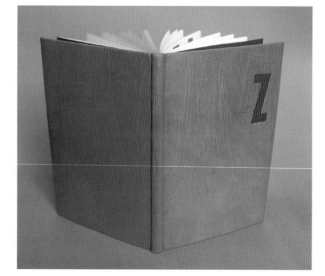

0176, 0177
Rebecca Chamlee,
Pie In The Sky Press,
USA

[0178
Elysia Lock, USA

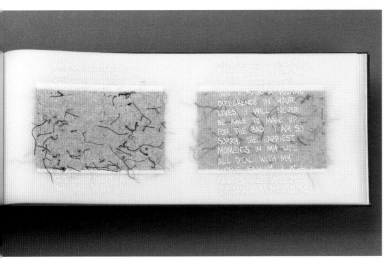

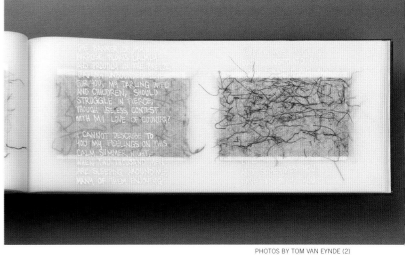

[0179, 0180
Jerry Bleem, USA

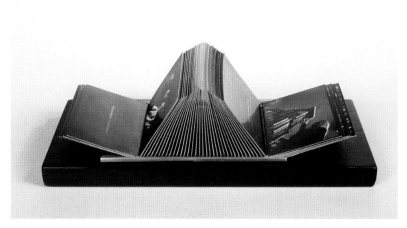

[0181, 0182
Betsy Davids, USA

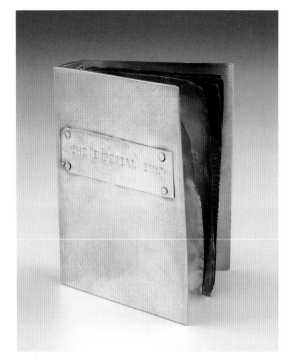

[0183, 0184
Jim Bové, USA

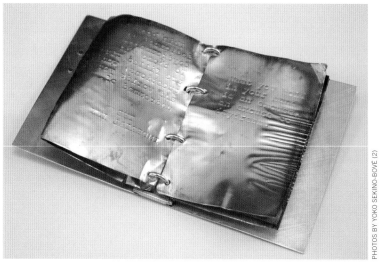

0185, 0186
Andrew Binder, USA

0187, 0188
Thomas Ingmire, Scriptorium St. Francis, USA

0189, 0190
Nancy A. Fiumera, The Studio at Far Enough, USA

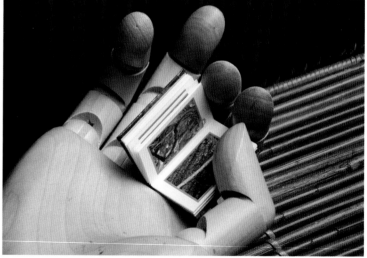

0191, 0192
Nancy A. Fiumera, The Studio at Far Enough, USA

PHOTOS BY C. KOOPMANN PHOTOGRAPHY (2)

0193, 0194

Barbara Brear, BB Miniatures, SOUTH AFRICA

PHOTOS BY C. KOOPMANN PHOTOGRAPHY (2)

0195, 0196

Barbara Brear, BB Miniatures, SOUTH AFRICA

0197, 0198
Miyako Akai, Kototsubo, JAPAN

0199
Madelyn Garrett, USA

0200, 0201, 0202
Richard Minsky, USA

PHOTO BY JENNIFER KENNARD

0203

Margery S. Hellmann,
The Holburne Press, USA

0204, 0205, 0206

Frank Hamrick,
Old Fan Press, USA

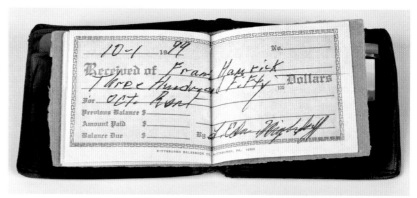

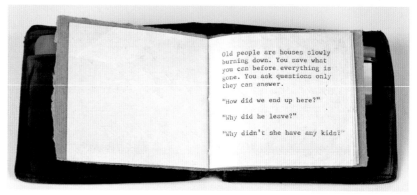

Old people are houses slowly
burning down. You save what
you can before everything is
gone. You ask questions only
they can answer.

"How did we end up here?"

"Why did he leave?"

"Why didn't she have any kids?"

0207, 0208
Lauren Henkin, Vela Noche, USA

0209
Marvel Grégoire, USA

INGTON, INDIANA. PHOTOS BY BILL BACHHUBER (2)

[0210, 0211
  Anne G. Greenwood, USA

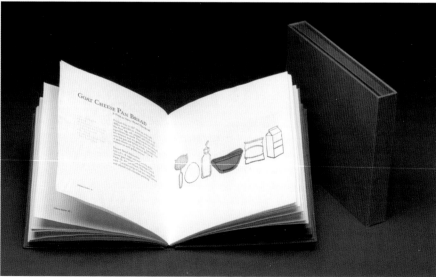

[0212
  **Annie E. Herlocker,
  Paper Revival Press**, USA

0213, 0214
Roberta Lavadour, Mission
Creek Press, USA

0215, 0216
Annie Fain Liden, A. Fain Books, USA

[0217, 0218
[**Kirsten Demer, Green Trike Press,** USA

0219, 0220, 0221
Mia Leijonstedt, UK

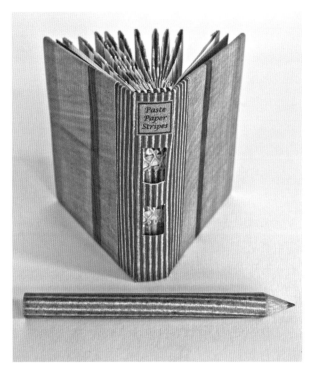

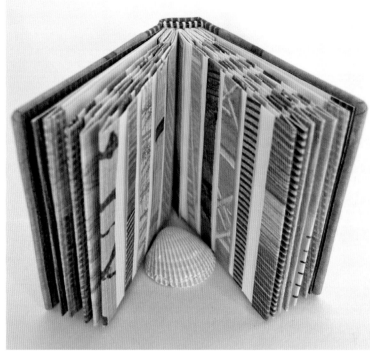

0222, 0223
Marie Kelzer, USA

0224
Sharon A. Sharp, Sharp Handmade
Books/Curious Pursuits Press, USA

0225, 0226
Marie Marcano, USA

0227, 0228
Kimberly Izenman, USA

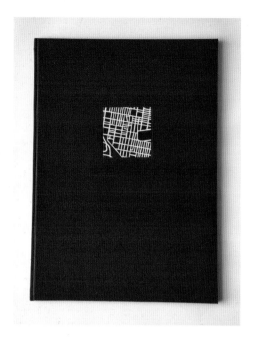

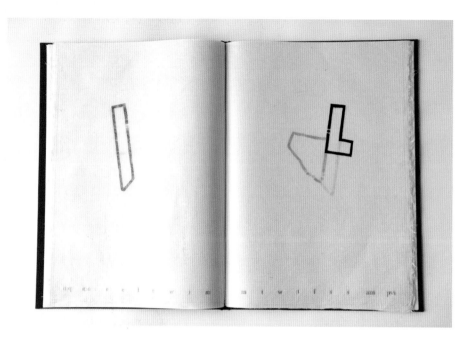

0229, 0230
Andrew Huot, Tank Dive Press, USA

0231
Ellen Knudson,
Crooked Letter Press, USA

0232, 0233, 0234

Thomas Ingmire,
Scriptorium St. Francis, USA

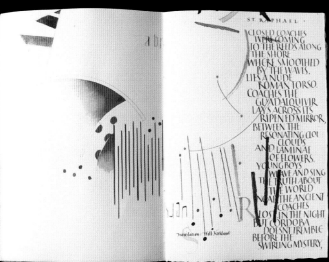

0235

Turner Hilliker, USA

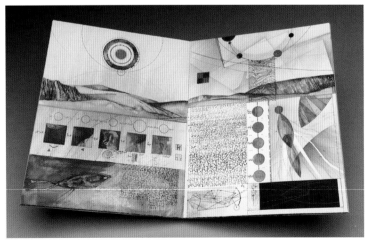
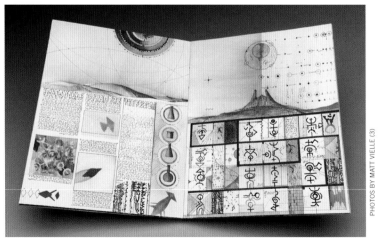

0236, 0237, 0238
Timothy C. Ely, USA

with reckless hearts and
summer haunted feet

0239, 0240, 0241
Nanette Wylde,
Hunger Rotten Books, USA

and we shall find the daisies
like a snow

0242
Beverly Ann Wilson, USA

PHOTO BY PAT BERRETT

0243, 0244
Julie Baugnet, USA

0245, 0246
Elizabeth Carls, USA

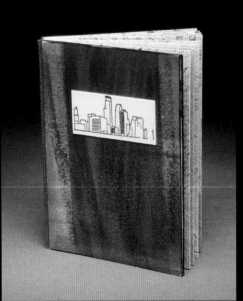

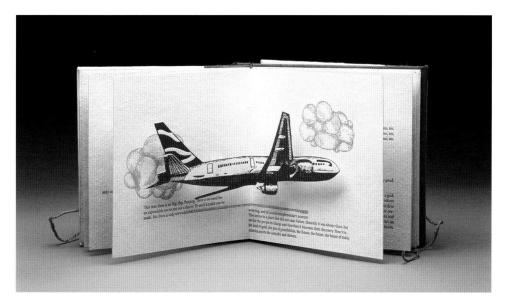

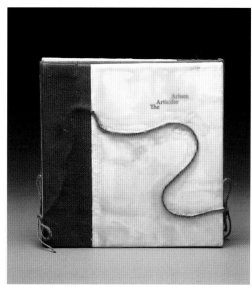

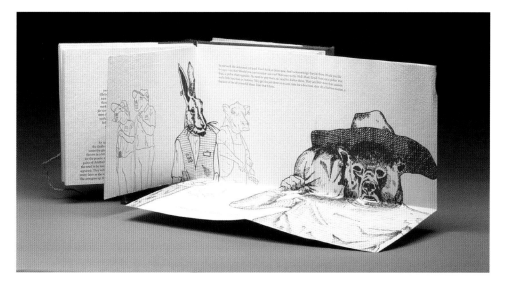

0247, 0248, 0249

Joseph Lappie,
Peptic Robots Press, USA

0250, 0251

Benjamin D. Rinehart,
USA

0252, 0253, 0254
Timothy C. Ely, USA

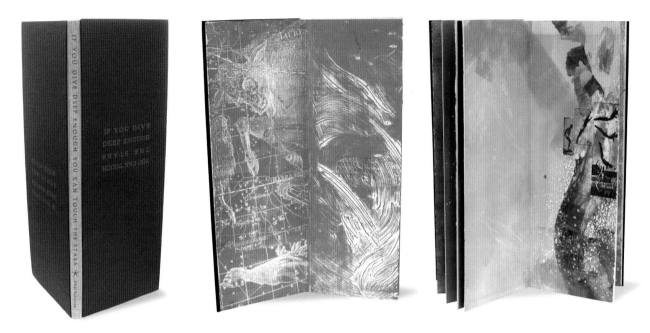

0255, 0256, 0257
Sibyl Rubottom, Bay Park Press, USA

0258, 0259
Mary Tasillo, Citizen Hydra Projects, USA

0260, 0261, 0262
Philip Zimmermann, USA

0263, 0264
Rae Trujillo, Raes of Sun, USA

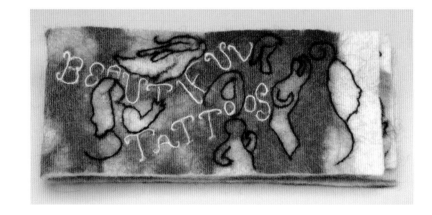

0265, 0266
Alisa Golden, never mind
the press, USA

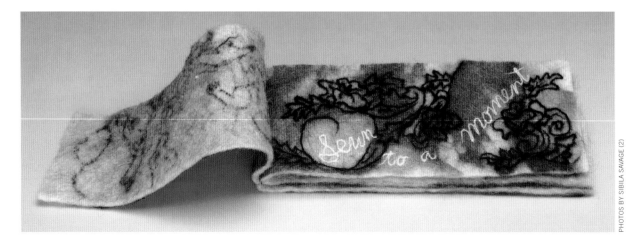

0267, 0268
Mo Orkiszewski, AUSTRALIA

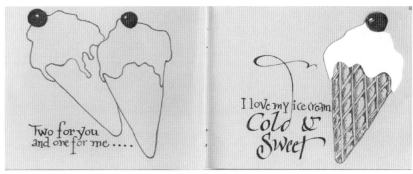

0269, 0270
Margaret Lammerts, CANADA

0271, 0272, 0273
Jan Owen, USA

0274
Terence Uren, AUSTRALIA

0275, 0276
Rutherford Witthus, φ (Phi Press), USA

0277
Dennis Yuen, USA

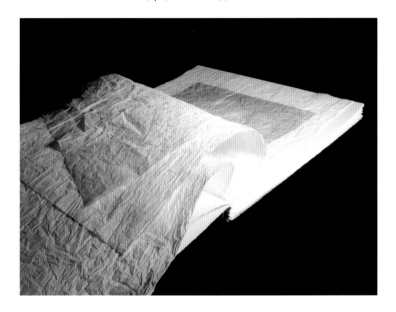

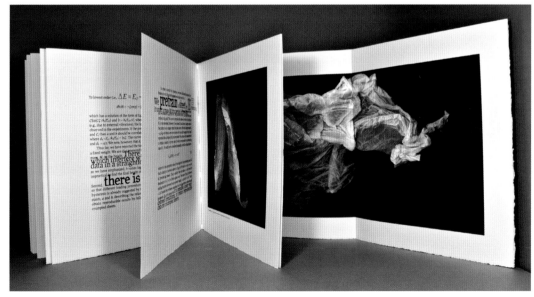

[0278, 0279
Beata Wehr, USA

[0280
Daniel Mayer, USA

[0281
Daniel Mayer, USA

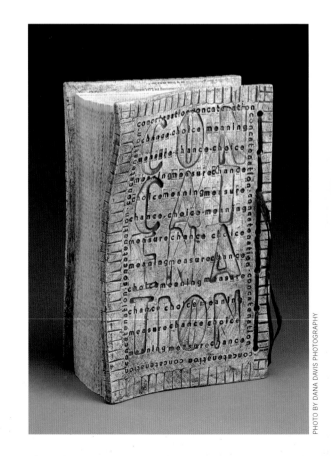

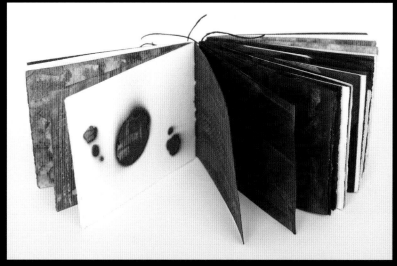

0282, 0283
Cindy Stiteler, USA

0284, 0285
Judith E. Strom, USA

[0286
Alis Olsen, USA

[0287, 0288
Mary Maynor, USA

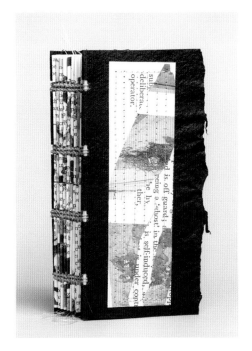

0289, 0290
Lin Max, USA

0291, 0292
Ellen Gradman, USA

0293
Dennis Yuen, USA

0297, 0298
Richard Troncone, USA

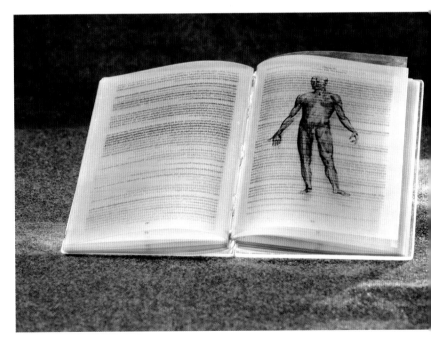

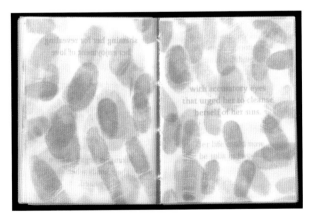

0294, 0295, 0296
Jennifer Hines, USA

0299
Hilke Kurzke, Büchertiger
Studio & Press, GERMANY

0300, 0301, 0302
Kent Manske, USA

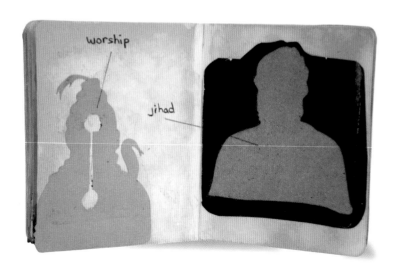

0303, 0304
Hedi Kyle, USA

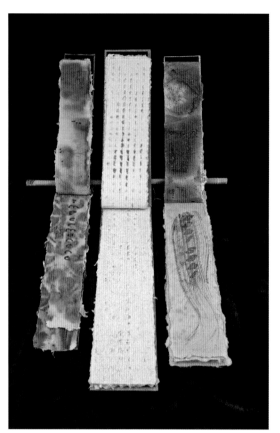

0305, 0306
Suzanne S. Hall, USA

0307, 0308
Dave Buchen, PUERTO RICO

It is impossible to imagine,
but the fowls did not only not come at the corn
but they forsook all that part of the island,
and I could never see a bird near the place
as long as my scarecrows hung there

0309, 0310
Bryson Dean-Gauthier, USA

0311
Helen Malone, AUSTRALIA

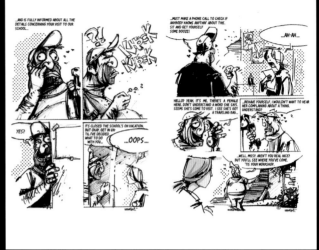

0312, 0313

Melissa Hilliard Potter, USA

0314, 0315

Barbara Simler, CANADA

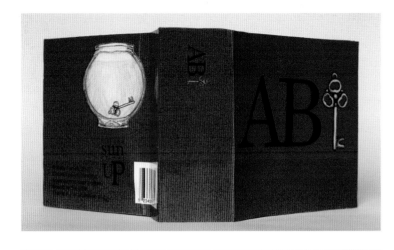

0316, 0317, 0318
Kelly Parsell, USA

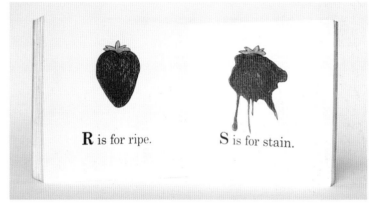

0319, 0320
Felicia Rice, Moving Parts Press, USA

PHOTO BY VICTORIA HINDLEY

PHOTO BY VICTORIA HINDLEY

PHOTO BY THE ARTIST

0321, 0322, 0323
Madelyn Garrett, USA

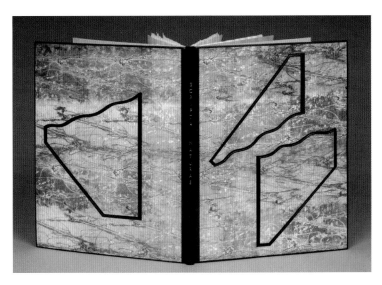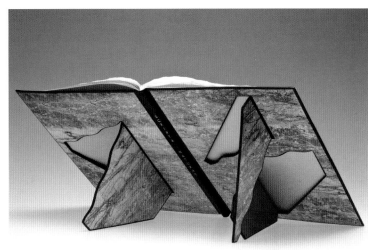

0324, 0325
Eleanore E. Ramsey, Eleanore E. Ramsey Design
Bookbinding, USA

0326
Jan Sobota, CZECH REPUBLIC

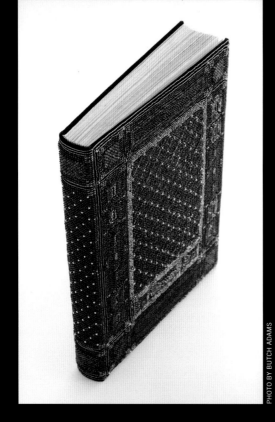

0327

Madelyn Garrett,
USA

0328

Cynthia Colbert, USA

0331, 0332
Karen Hanmer, USA

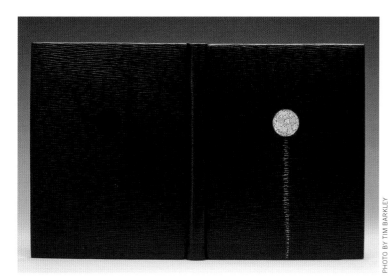

0333
Monique Lallier, USA

PHOTO BY TIM BARKLEY

0334
Richard Kegler, USA

[0335
Richard Minsky, USA

[0336, 0337
Daniel E. Kelm, Wide Awake Garage, USA

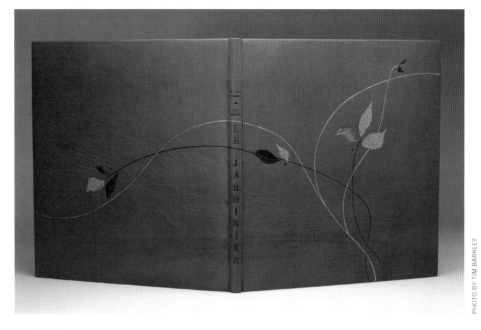

0338
Cynthia Colbert, USA

0339
Monique Lallier, USA

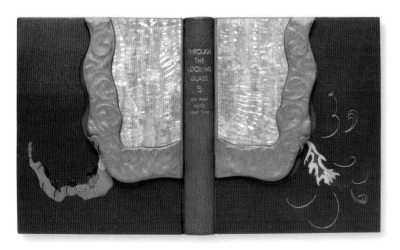

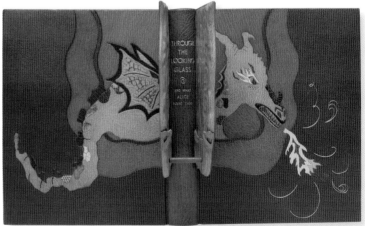

0340, 0341
**Eleanore E. Ramsey, Eleanore E. Ramsey Design
Bookbinding**, USA

0342, 0343

Robert Walp, Chester Creek Press, USA

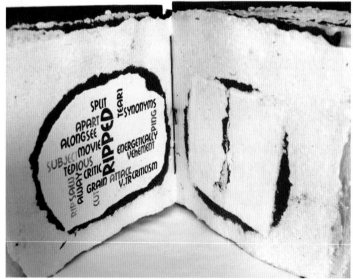

0344, 0345

Gail Stiffe, Hands on Paper, AUSTRALIA

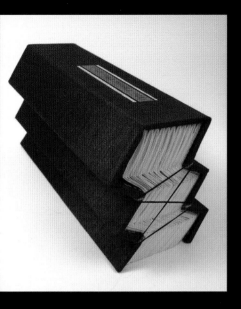

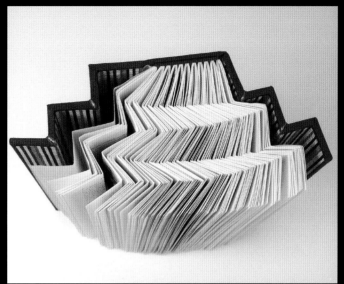

0346, 0347
Peggy Johnston, Waveland Studio, USA

0348, 0349
Debbie Hill, AUSTRALIA

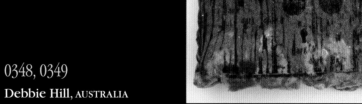

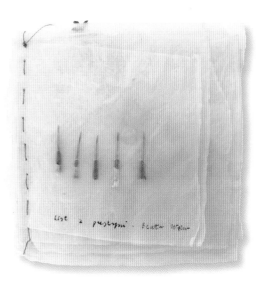

[0350, 0351
Beata Wehr, USA

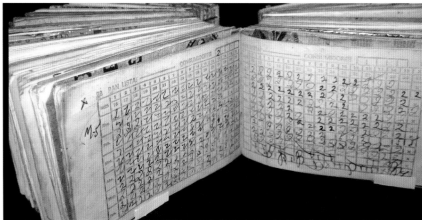

[0352, 0353
Steven C. Dauber,
Red Trillium Press, USA

0354
Dolph Smith, USA

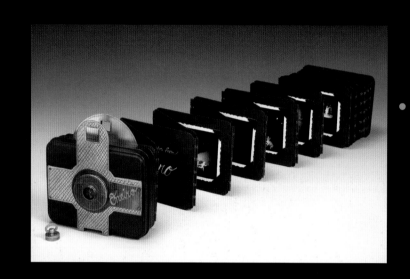

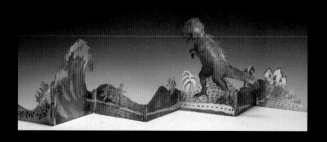

Chapter 2:
ACCORDION AND FOLDABLE BOOKS
books with multiple-fold pages

Books made with pleated pages
or having pleated covers:

- accordion books, flag books,
  Jacob's ladder books

Books with multiple sets of pleated pages
attached to covers:

- tunnel books, carousel/star books

Books with multiple-fold pages:

- origami books, gate-fold books,
  map-fold books, maze books, flexagons

0355–0637

0355
Hedi Kyle, USA

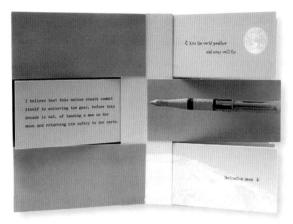

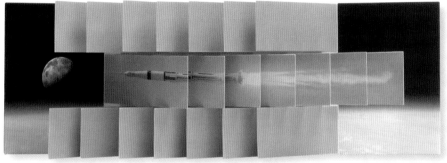

0356, 0357, 0358
Karen Hanmer, USA

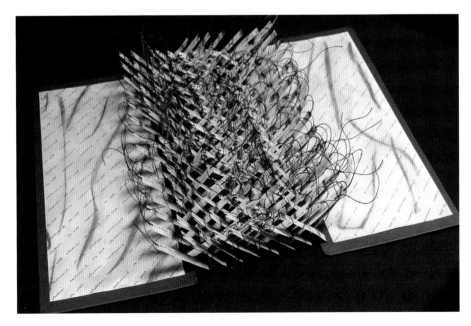

0359
C J. Shane, USA

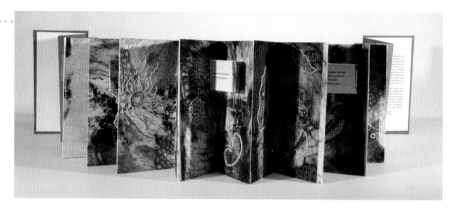

0360, 0361

Michelle Wilson,
Rocinante Press, USA

0362, 0363

Alice Simpson, USA

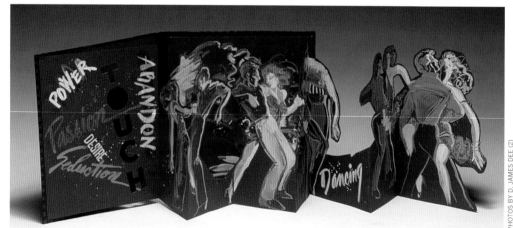

0364

Laura Russell,
Simply Books, Ltd., USA

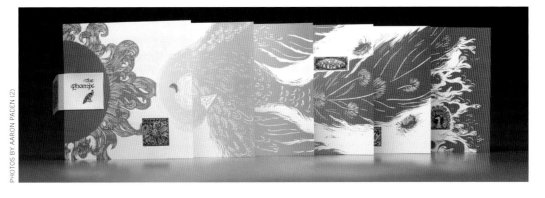

0365, 0366

Linda Samson-Talleur,
La Ginestra, USA

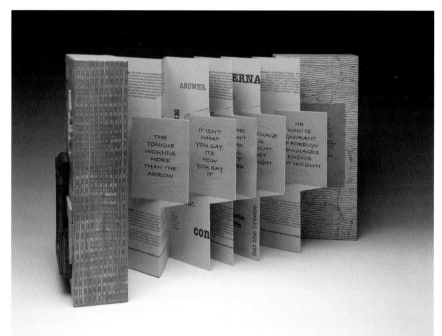

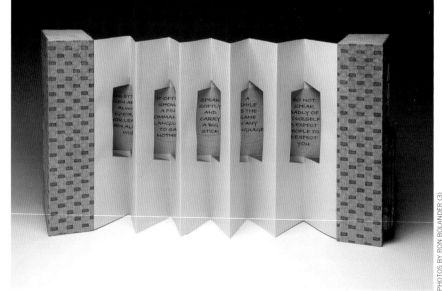

0367, 0368, 0369

Jackie Gardener, USA

0370, 0371, 0372
Laura Russell,
Simply Books, Ltd., USA

0373
Sammy Lee, Studio SML/K, USA

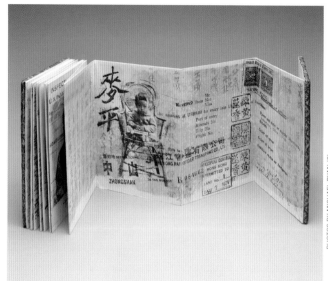

PHOTOS BY MICHAEL RYAN (2)

[0374, 0375
[MalPina Chan, USA

[0376
[Opie and Linda O'Brien,
[Burnt Offerings Studio, USA

PHOTO BY DINA ROSSI

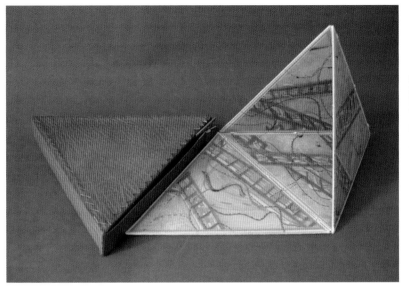

0377
Mary Laird, Quelque fois Press, USA

0378
Pamela S. Gibson, ThistlePaper Press, USA

0379
Marama Warren,
The Creative Spirit, AUSTRALIA

0380
Robyn A. Daniel,
USA

0381, 0382
Alice Austin, Artist Books, USA

0383, 0384
Opie and Linda O'Brien,
Burnt Offerings Studio, USA

0385, 0386
Maddy Rosenberg, USA

0387, 0388
Bea Nettles, USA

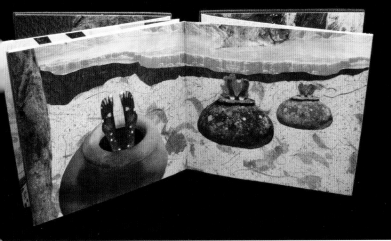

0389, 0390, 0391
Dorothy Simpson Krause,
Viewpoint Editions, USA

0392
Sue Huggins Leopard,
Leopard Studio Editions, USA

0393, 0394, 0395
Opie and Linda O'Brien, Burnt Offerings Studio, USA

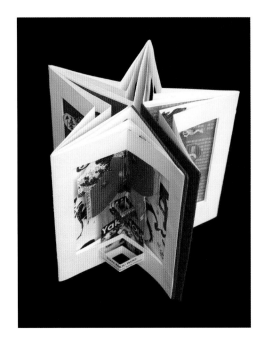

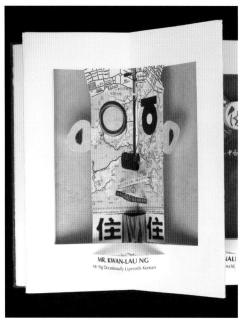

0396, 0397, 0398
Rachelle W. Chuang, Rachelle W. Chuang Art & Design, USA

0399
Roberta Lavadour,
Mission Creek Press, USA

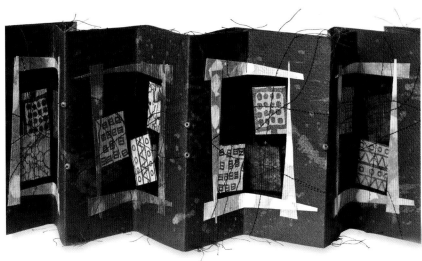

0400, 0401
Barbara Bussolari, USA

0402
Mary V. Marsh,
Quite Contrary Press, USA

0403
Bea Nettles, USA

0404, 0405
Béatrice Coron, USA

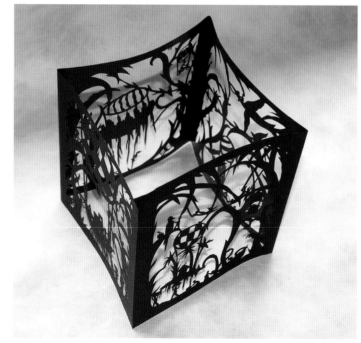

PHOTOS BY MELISSA OLEN (2)

0406, 0407

Sarah Bodman, Bookarts at the
Centre for Fine Print Research, UK

0408, 0409

Dea Fischer, rock-paper-scissors, CANADA

0410, 0411, 0412
Elizabeth Beronich Sheets, USA

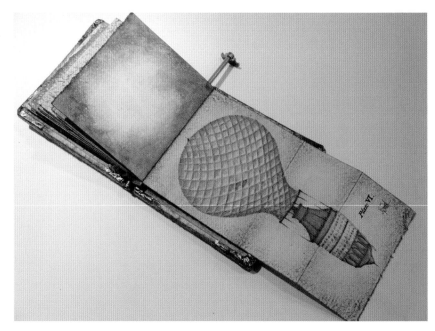

0413, 0414, 0415
Elizabeth Beronich Sheets, USA

0416
Susan Mackin Dolan, USA

0417, 0418
Maddy Rosenberg,
USA

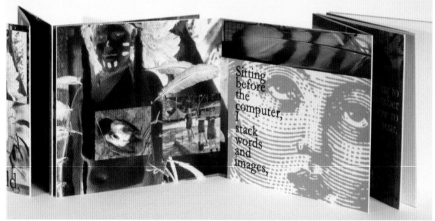

0419, 0420
Deborah Kogan, USA

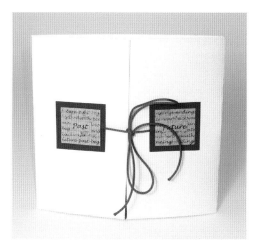

0421, 0422

Evelyn Eller Rosenbaum, USA

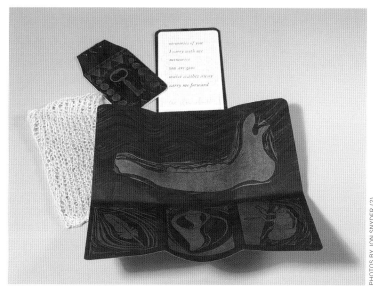

0423, 0424

Alice Austin, Artist Books, USA

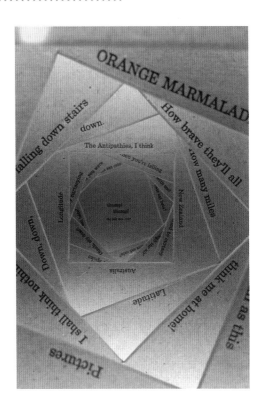

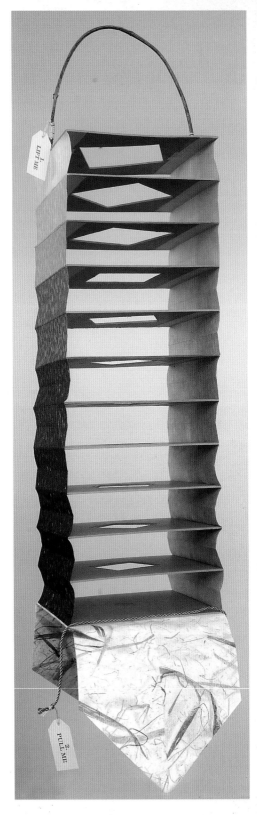

0425, 0426, 0427

Tara Bryan,
walking bird press, CANADA

0428

Bettina Pauly, USA

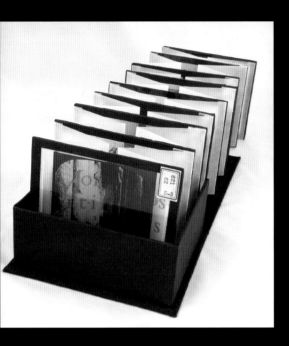

0429, 0430
Margaret Suchland, USA

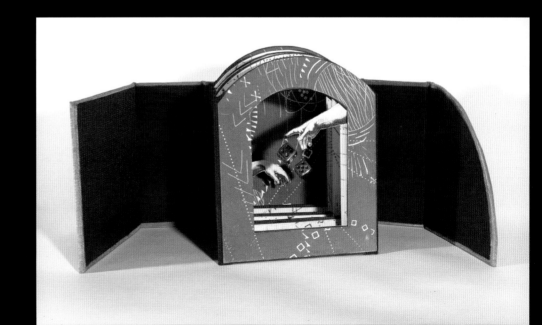

0431
Ruth Bardenstein, USA

0432, 0433
Patricia Sarrafian Ward, USA

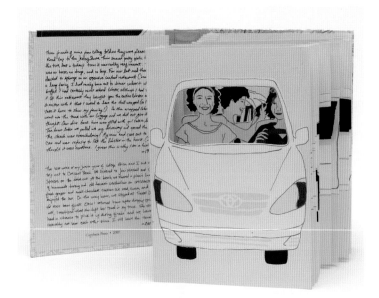

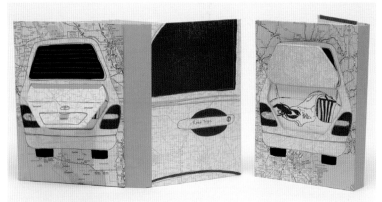

0434, 0435
Ashley L. Schick, USA

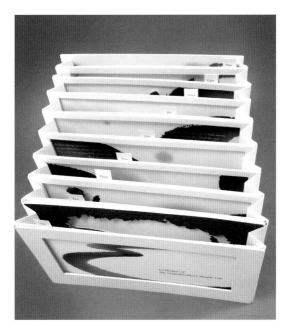

0436, 0437
Sun Young Kang, USA

0438
Jana Sim, USA

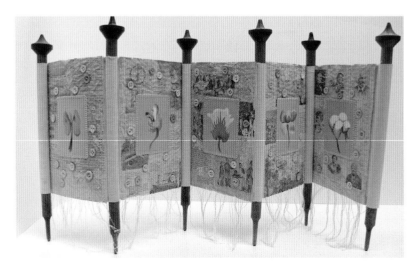

PHOTO BY CHRISTOPHER CAMPBELL

0443
Elissa R. Campbell, Blue Roof Designs, USA

0444
Alice Stanne,
USA

0445, 0446
Renee Jarmolowicz, Artist Alcove, USA

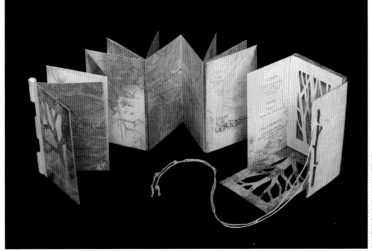

PHOTOS BY SASHA WALKER (2)

0447, 0448
Eleonora Cumer, ITALY

0449, 0450
Arlyn Ende, USA

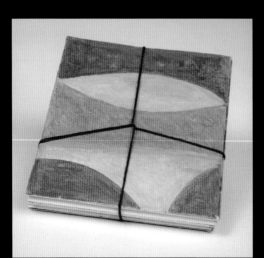

0451, 0452
Fiona Merridew, USA

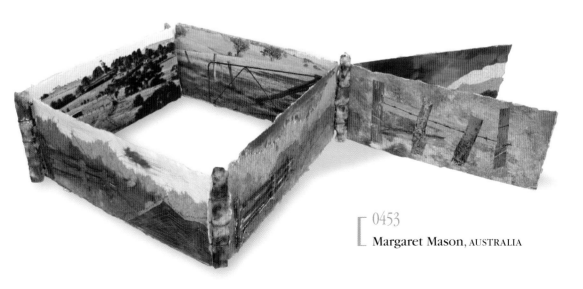

0453
Margaret Mason, AUSTRALIA

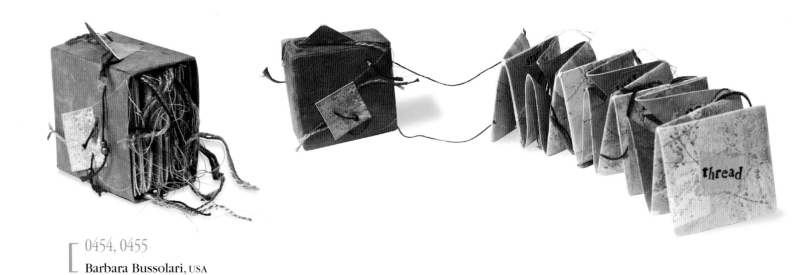

0454, 0455
Barbara Bussolari, USA

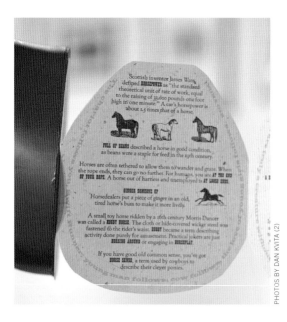

0456, 0457
Jessica Spring, Springtide Press, USA

0459
Helen Sanderson, AUSTRALIA

0458
Eriko Takahashi, USA

0460
Margaret Suchland, USA

PHOTO BY JAY SUCHLAND

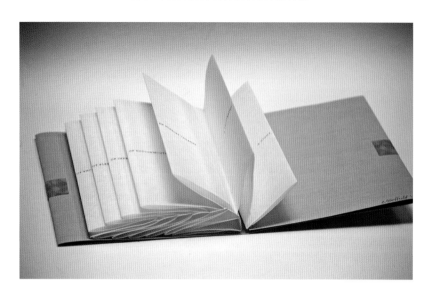

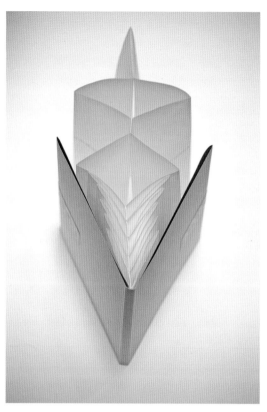

0461, 0462
Ellen Sheffield, Unit IV Arts, USA

0463
Judith Hoffman, USA

0464, 0465
Cathy Ryan, USA

0466, 0467
Susan Makov, Green Cat Press, USA

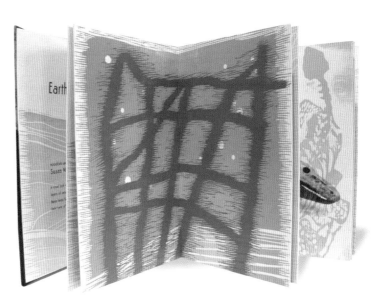

0468, 0469

Bridget R. O'Donnell,
USA

0470, 0471, 0472

Ellen Sheffield, Unit IV Arts, USA

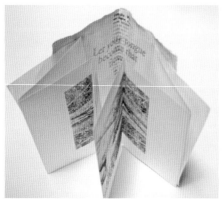

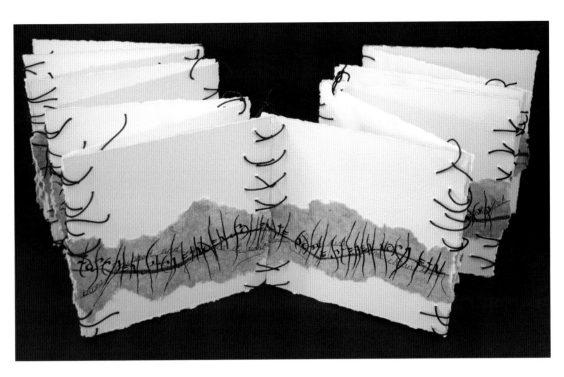

[0473
Kay Byrne, REPUBLIC OF IRELAND

[0474
Jerry Bleem, USA

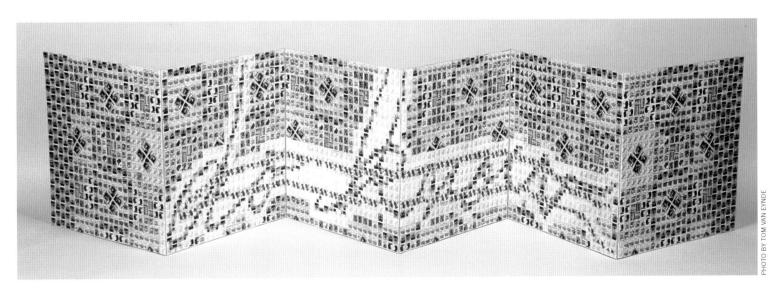

PHOTO BY TOM VAN EYNDE

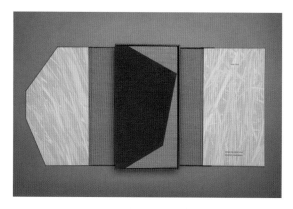

PHOTOS BY SIBILA SAVAGE (3)

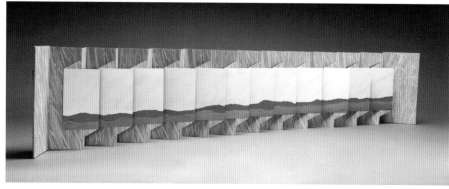

[0475, 0476, 0477
  Julie Chen, Flying Fish Press, USA

[0478
  Maria G. Pisano,
  Memory Press, USA

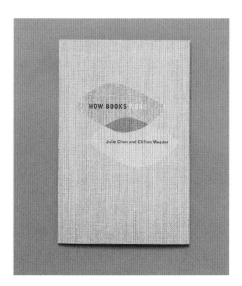

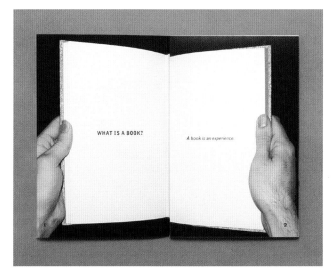

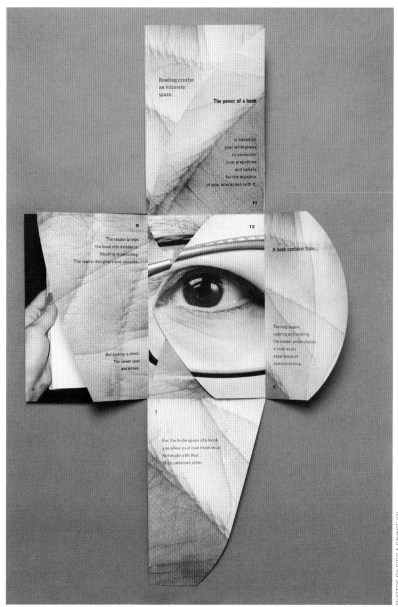

0479, 0480, 0481

**Julie Chen, Flying Fish Press;
Clifton Meador,** USA

0482, 0483
Karen Kunc,
Blue Heron Press, USA

0484
Lawrence G. Van Veleer,
Peggy Gotthold,
Foolscap Press, USA

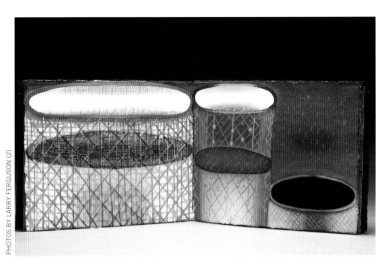
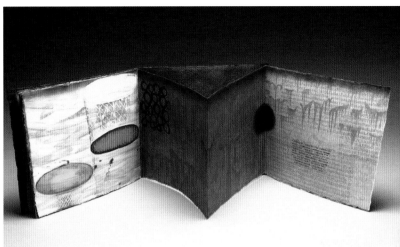

0485, 0486
Karen Kunc, Blue Heron Press, USA

0487
Ginger Burrell, Midnight Moon Press, USA

┌ 0488
└ **Amandine Nabarra-Piomelli,** USA

┌ 0489, 0490
└ **Ann Lovett,** USA

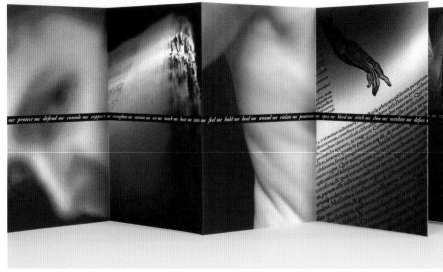

PHOTOS BY SHAWN LINEHAN (2)

[0491, 0492
Mary Beth Boone, USA

[0493, 0494
Ann Lovett, USA

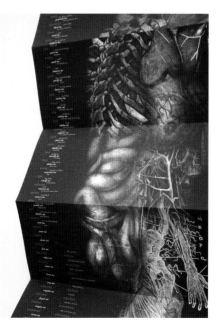
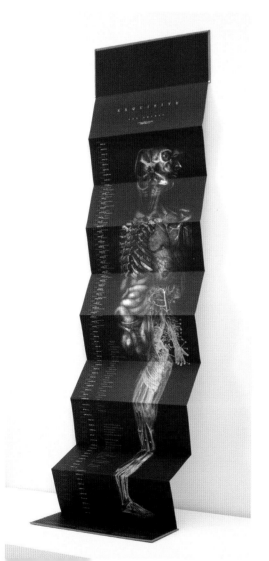

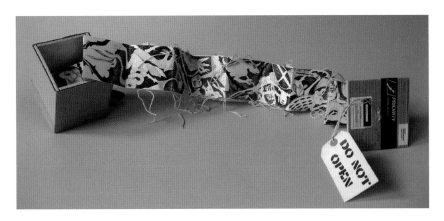

0495
Fran Watson, USA

0496
Cathy DeForest,
Jubilation Press, USA

0497, 0498
Cathy Ryan, USA

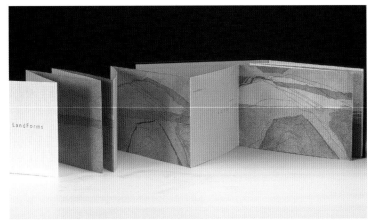

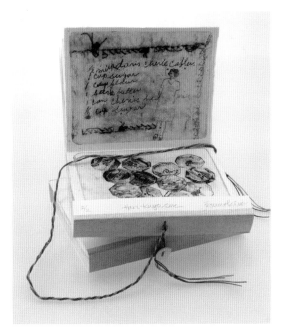

0499, 0500
Juanita H. Tumelaire, Impmaker Press, USA

0501, 0502
Charlotte Hedlund, USA

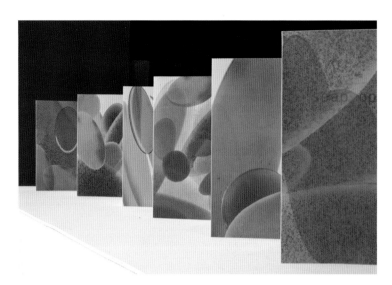
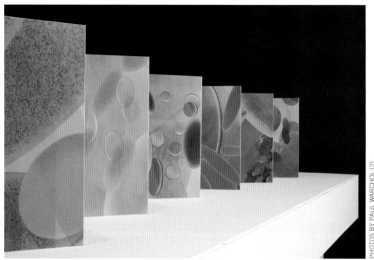

[0503, 0504
Hedi Kyle, USA

[0505
Lisa Hasegawa, ilfant press, USA

[0506
Sibyl Rubottom, Bay Park Press, USA

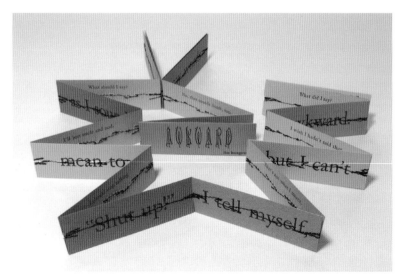

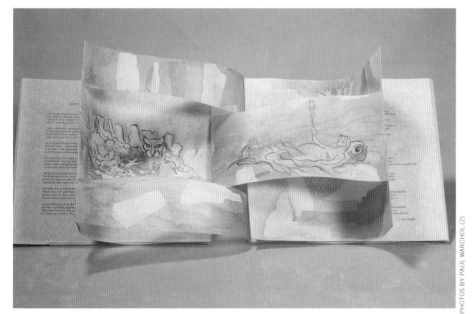

0507, 0508
Hedi Kyle, USA

0509, 0510
Isabelle Faivre, FRANCE

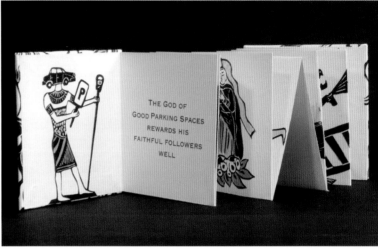

0511, 0512
Jenny Craig, Notta Pixie Press, USA

0513, 0514
Dayle Doroshow,
Zingaro, USA

0515, 0516

Art Hazelwood, USA

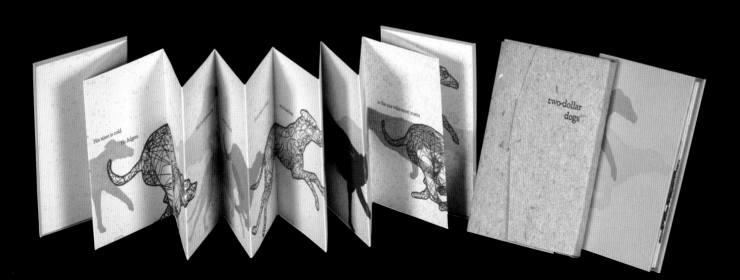

0517

Lauren Faulkenberry Firebrand Press, USA

0518, 0519
Alicia Griswold, USA

0520
Elizabeth Holster, USA

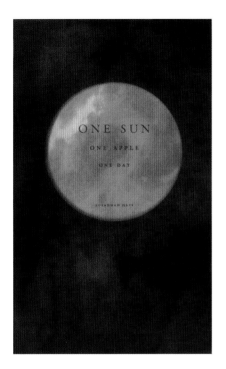

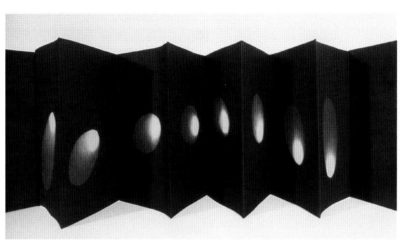

0521, 0522
Susannah Hays, Venus Pencils, USA

0523, 0524
Roni Gross, Z'roah Press, USA

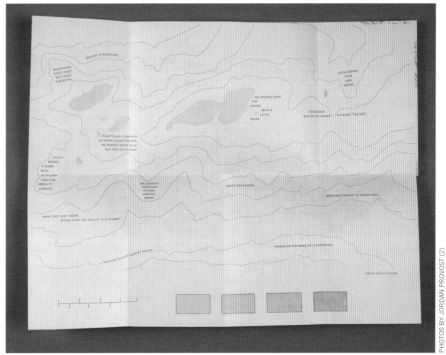

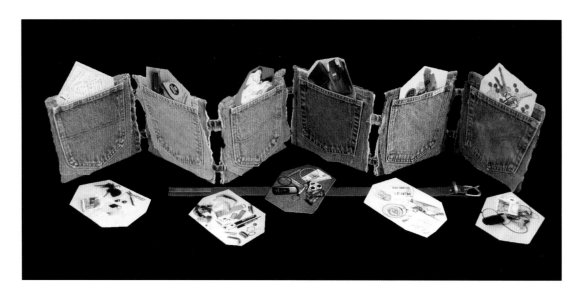

[0525
Ginger Burrell, Midnight Moon Press, USA

[0526, 0527
Amanda D'Amico, USA

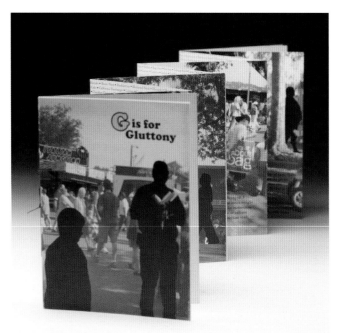

0528, 0529, 0530

Pien Rotterdam,
Water Leaf Press, THE NETHERLANDS

0531

Jeanne Germani, CANADA

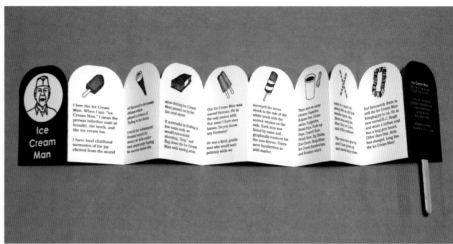

0532, 0533
Michael A. Henninger, Rat Art Press, USA

0534
Annette Geistfeld, USA

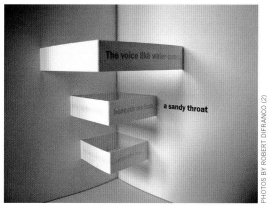

[0535, 0536
Warren K. Buss, Naos Press, USA

[0537
Marvel Grégoire, USA

[0538
Jackie Gardener, USA

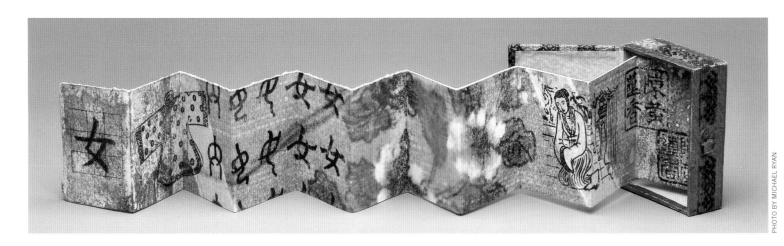

0539
MalPina Chan, USA

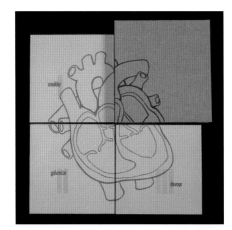

0540, 0541, 0542
Lauren Faulkenberry,
Firebrand Press, USA

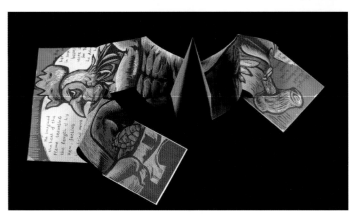

0543
Carly Drew, USA

0544, 0545
Cari Ferraro, USA

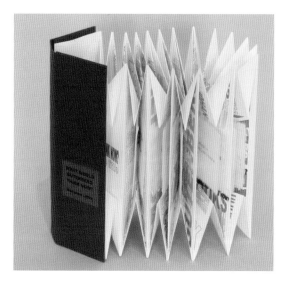

0546, 0547
Marianne Little, AUSTRALIA

0548
Suzanne Lydia Weinert, USA

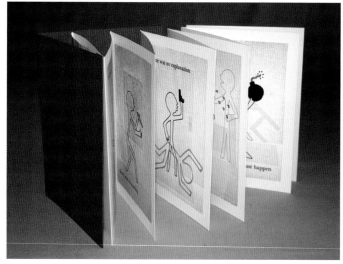

0549
Emily Martin, Naughty Dog Press, USA

0550, 0551
Kirsten Demer, Green Trike Press, USA

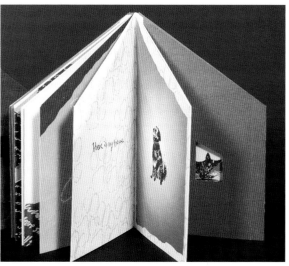

0552, 0553
Eriko Takahashi, USA

0554, 0555
Sarah Vogel, Slow Industries, USA

0556
Andrew Huot, Tank Dive Press, USA

0557, 0558
Lesley Mitchell, Luminous Unit Press, USA

0559
Lisa McGarry, ITALY

0560
Barbara Johnston, CANADA

0561, 0562, 0563
Kestutis Vasiliunas, LITHUANIA

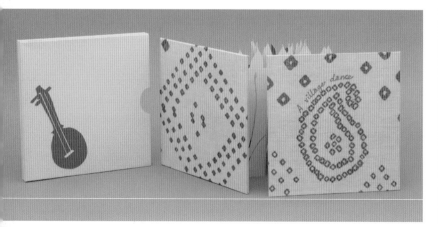

0564, 0565
Bhavna Mehta, Hansa Arts, USA

[0566, 0567
Lin Max, USA

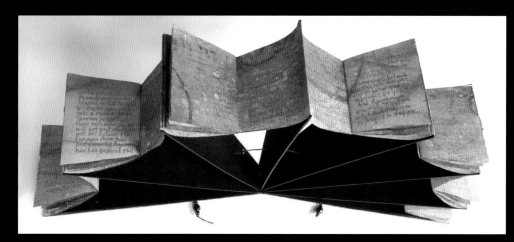

[0568, 0569
Gail Prostrollo, USA

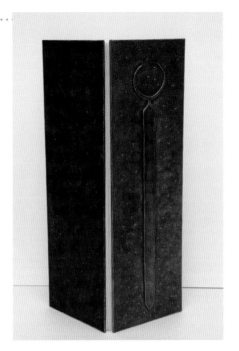

0570, 0571
Marlis Maehrle, GERMANY

0572, 0573
Helen Malone, AUSTRALIA

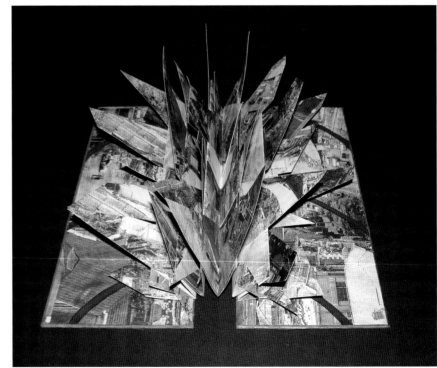

0574, 0575
Catherine Nash, USA

0576
Mary Maynor, USA

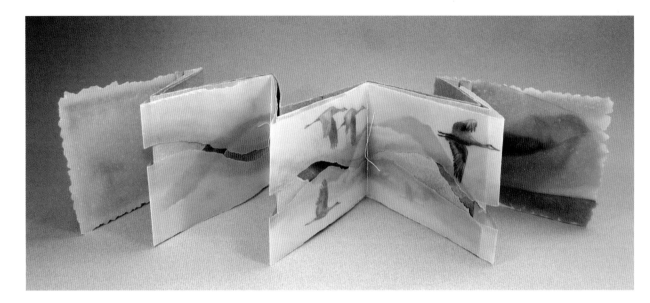

0577
Margy O'Brien,
USA

0578, 0579
Sandy Webster, USA

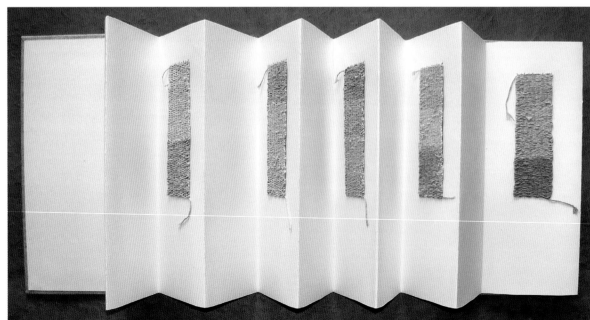

0580, 0581
Jen Thomas, Veronica Press, USA

0582, 0583
Sandra Winkworth, AUSTRALIA

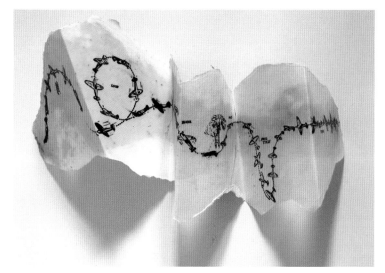

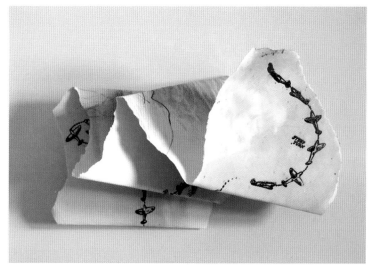

0584, 0585, 0586
Lynn Skordal, USA

0587, 0588
Alice Armstrong,
Flotsam Studio, USA

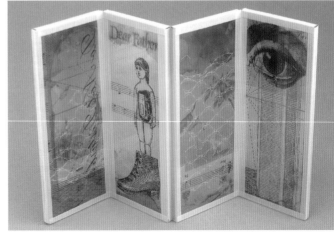

0589, 0590
Lynn Skordal, USA

0591, 0592
Beverly Ann Wilson, USA

0593, 0594, 0595
Mary Tasillo, Citizen Hydra Projects, USA

0596
Jill Timm,
Mystical Places Press, USA

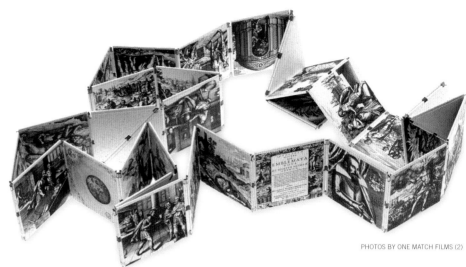

PHOTOS BY ONE MATCH FILMS (2)

0597, 0598
Daniel E. Kelm, Wide Awake Garage, USA

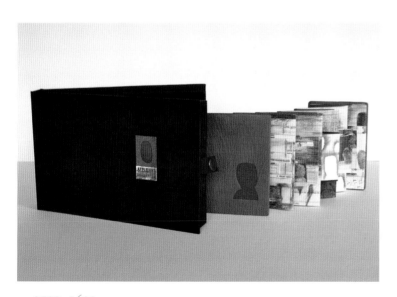

0599, 0600
Paulette Rosen, USA

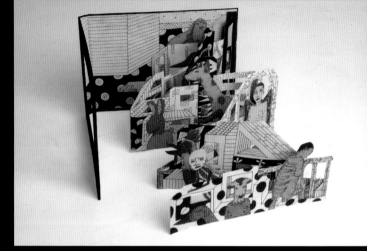

0601, 0602, 0603
Eunkang Koh, USA

0604
Elizabeth Holster,
USA

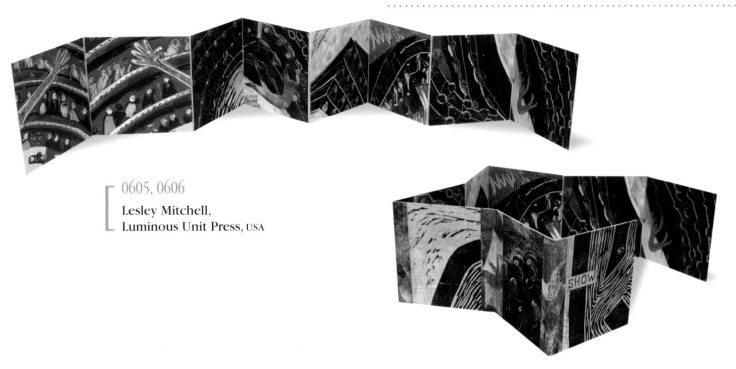

0605, 0606

Lesley Mitchell,
Luminous Unit Press, USA

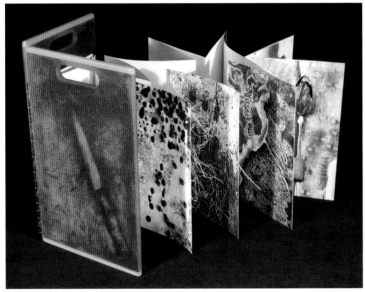

0607

Hanne Niederhausen, USA

0608

Anna Mavromatis, USA

0609, 0610

Purgatory Pie Press, Dikko Faust + Esther K Smith, collaborating artist: Bill Fick, USA

0611

Marilyn Stablein, USA

0612

Vicki Smith, USA

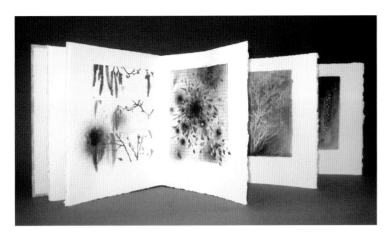

0613, 0614
Andie Thrams, USA

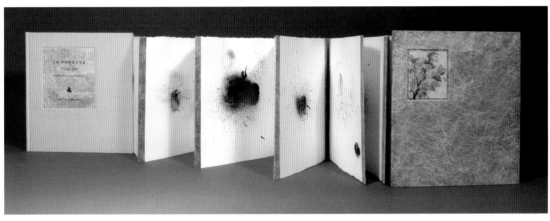

0615, 0616
Kevin Steele, USA

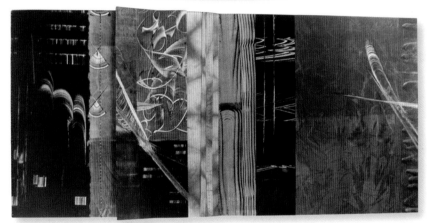

0617, 0618
Anna Mavromatis,
USA

0619, 0620
Mary McCarthy, USA

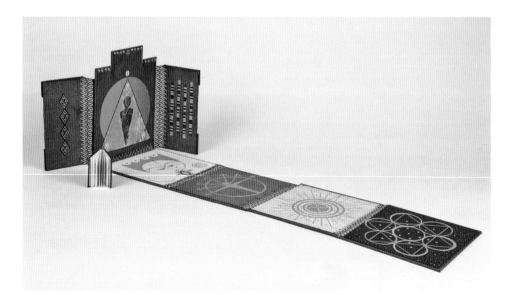

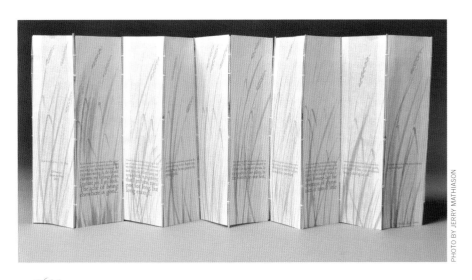

PHOTO BY JERRY MATHIASON

0621
C.B. Sherlock, Seymour Press, USA

0622, 0623
Anastasia Weigle,
"In a Bind" Studio, USA

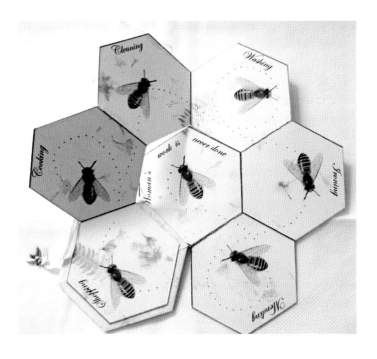

0624, 0625
Maria Winkler,
USA

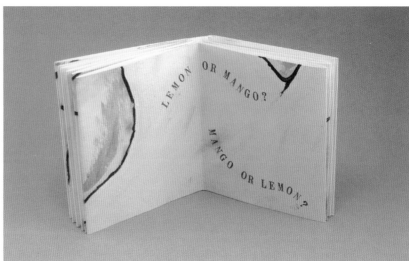

0626, 0627
Elaine G. Chu, USA

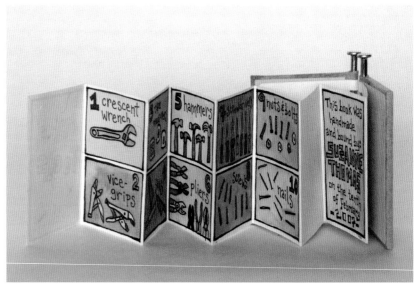

0628, 0629
Suzanne Lydia Weinert, USA

0630, 0631
Elena Mary Siff, USA

0632, 0633
Stephanie Wilde,
Smith and Wilde Press, USA

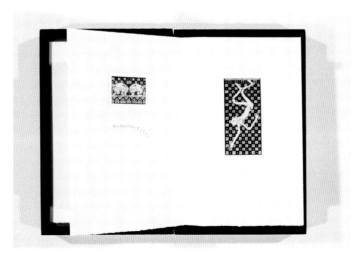

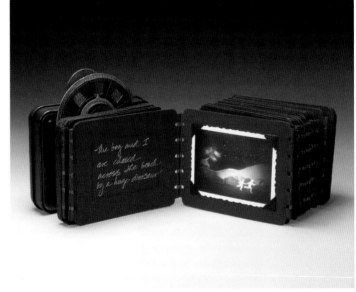

0634, 0635, 0636
Judith Hoffman, USA

0637
Peter & Donna Thomas, USA

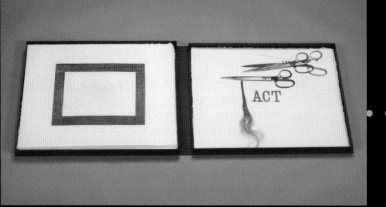

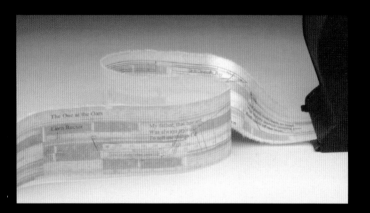

Chapter 3:
SINGLE-SHEET BOOKS
books with single-sheet pages

Books made with single-sheet pages
attached by a single fastener, staple
or sewing station:

- fan bindings, palm leaf books

Books made with single-sheet pages
placed in a container that acts as a cover:

- portfolio of prints, Tibetan books

Books made with single-sheet pages
rolled up:

- scrolls

0638–
0696

[0638, 0639

Eleonora Cumer, ITALY

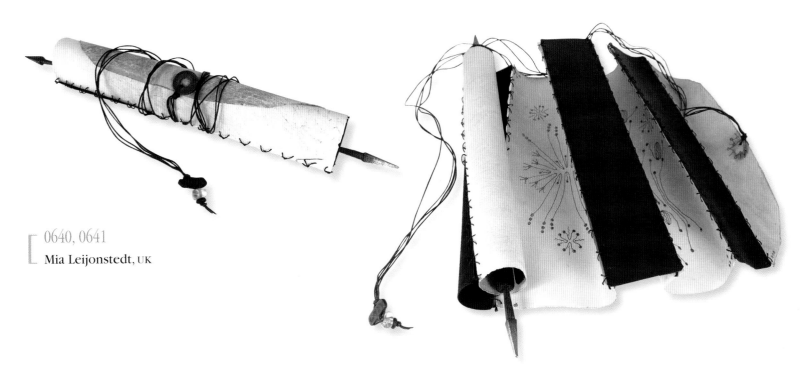

0640, 0641
Mia Leijonstedt, UK

0642, 0643
Matt Cohen, C & C Press, USA

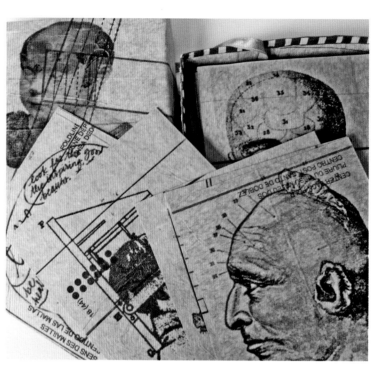

[0644, 0645
Sandra T. Donabed, Ganymede Studio, USA

[0646
Peter Madden, USA

0647, 0648
Rocco Scary, USA

0649, 0650, 0651
Mara Jevera Fulmer, USA

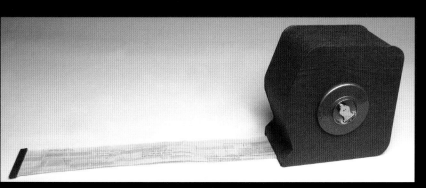

0652, 0653
Kerri Cushman,
performing goats press, USA

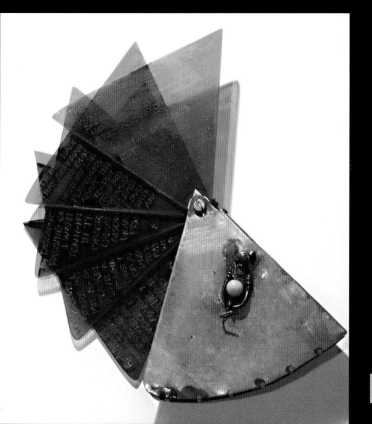

0655
Dorothy Field, CANADA

0654
Robert Roesch, USA

0656

Judith Serebrin,
Judith of Serebrin
Books & Prints, USA

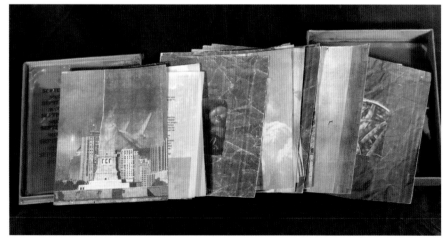

0657, 0658

Dorothy Field, CANADA

0659, 0660
Judith Serebrin,
Judith of Serebrin Books & Prints, USA

0661, 0662
Amandine Nabarra-Piomelli, USA

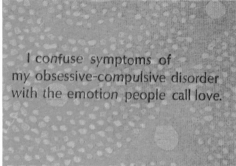

I confuse symptoms of
my obsessive-compulsive disorder
with the emotion people call love.

I latch on and I don't let go.

0663, 0664, 0665
Sarah Nicholls, USA

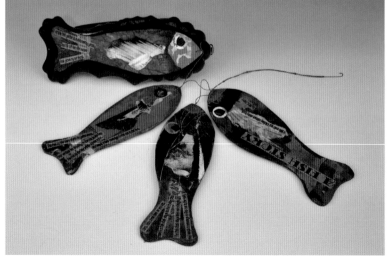

0666, 0667
Jill K. Berry, USA

0668, 0669
Guylaine Couture, CANADA

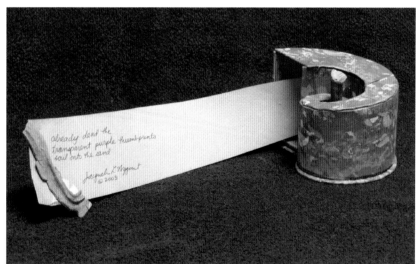

0670, 0671
Jacqueline L. Wygant, One O.A.K. Book Arts, USA

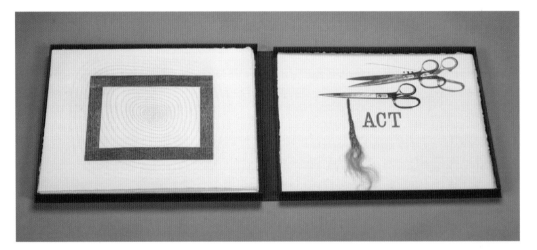

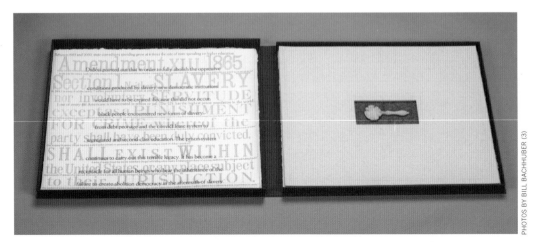

0672, 0673, 0674
Diane Jacobs,
Scantron Press, USA

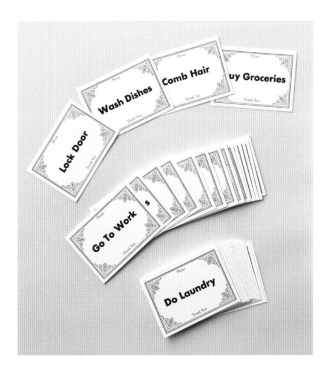

0675
Andrew Huot, Tank Dive Press, USA

0676
Suzanne Reese Horvitz, USA

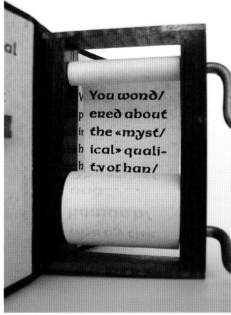

0677, 0678
Peter & Donna Thomas,
USA

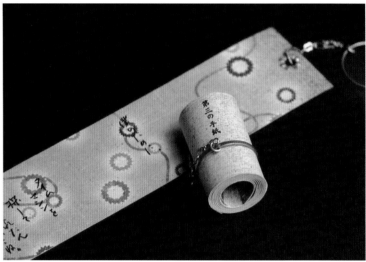

0679, 0680
Miyako Akai, Kototsubo, JAPAN

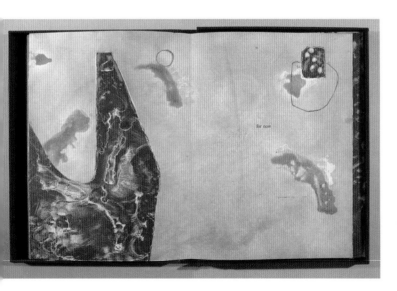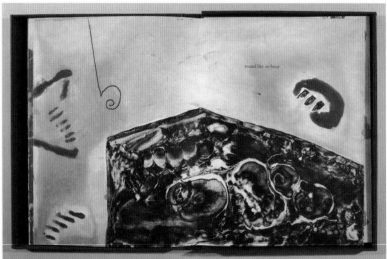

0681, 0682
Sarah Plimpton, USA

PHOTO BY GRACE CLARK RODICH

[0683
Friedrich Kerksieck,
Small Fires Press, USA

PHOTO BY TIM GURCZAK

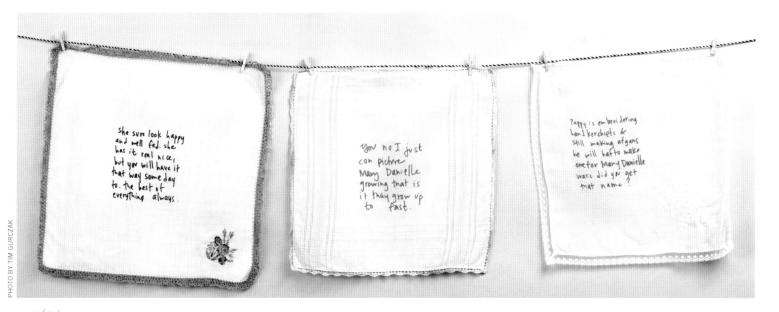

she sure look happy
and well fed. she
has it real nice,
but you will have it
that way some day
to. the best of
everything always.

You no I just
can picture
Mary Danielle
growing that is
it thay grow up
to fast.

Pappy is embroidering
handkerchiefs &
still making afgans
he will hafto make
one for Mary Danielle
ware did you get
that name?

[0684
Mary Goldthwaite-Gagne, USA

0685, 0686, 0687
Jana Sim, USA

0688
Steven C. Dauber,
Red Trillium Press, USA

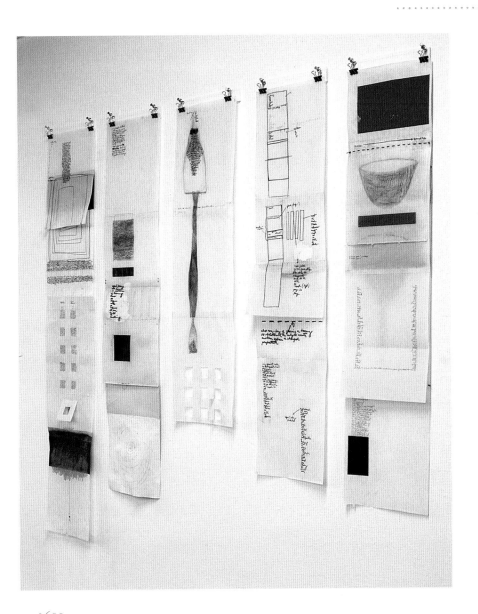

0689
Anne Gilman, USA

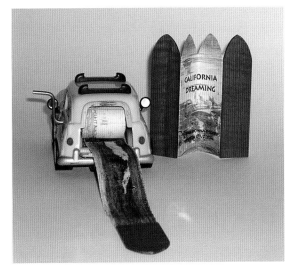

0690, 0691
Peter & Donna Thomas, USA

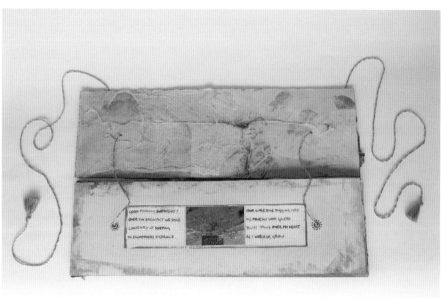

0692, 0693

Nina Judin, Nina Judin Books,
THE NETHERLANDS

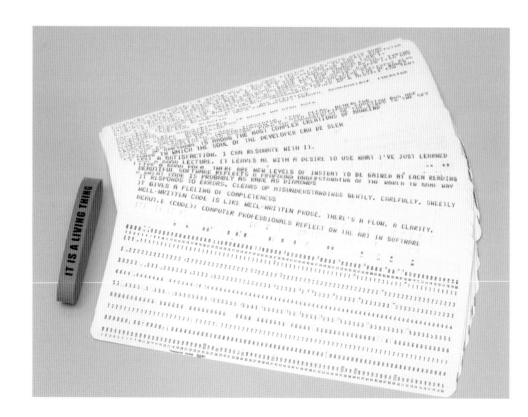

0694

Karen Hanmer,
USA

0695, 0696
Charlotte Hedlund, USA

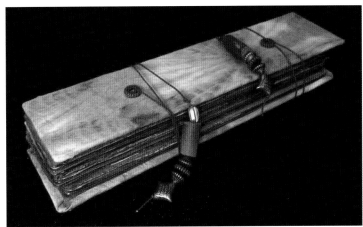

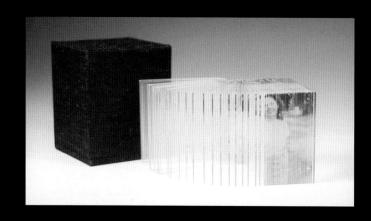

Chapter 4:
SCULPTURAL BOOKS

books made from objects
and objects made into books

Collections with at least one codex,
folded, or single-sheet book:

- shrines, reliquary, vessels, containers, etc.

Book-referential objects or book artworks:

- altered books, wearable books, edible,
  books, game boards, hinged blocks

Work referencing the intent, use,
or experience, etc. of books:

- installations, objects with letters on them,
  environmental books

$$\frac{0697}{1000}$$

0697

Jody Alexander, USA

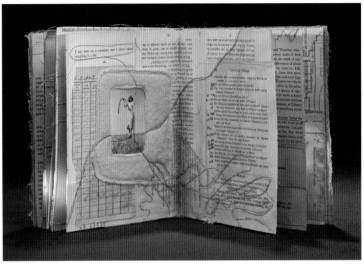

0698, 0699

Jody Alexander, USA

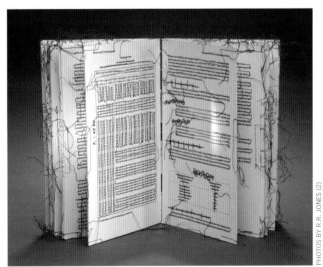

0700, 0701

Jody Alexander, USA

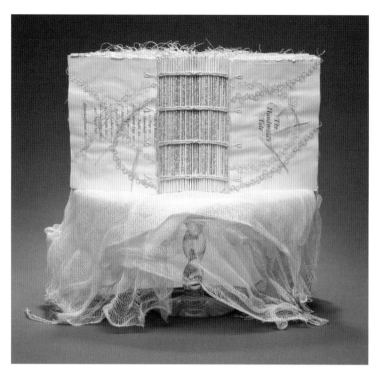

[0702, 0703
Jody Alexander, USA

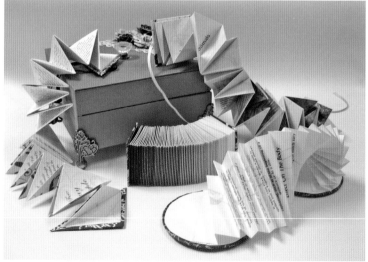

[0704, 0705
Patricia Grass, Green Heron Book Arts, USA

0706
Béatrice Coron, USA

0707, 0708
Susan Porteous, USA

0709, 0710, 0711, 0712, 0713, 0714

Laurie Corral, BookWorks, USA

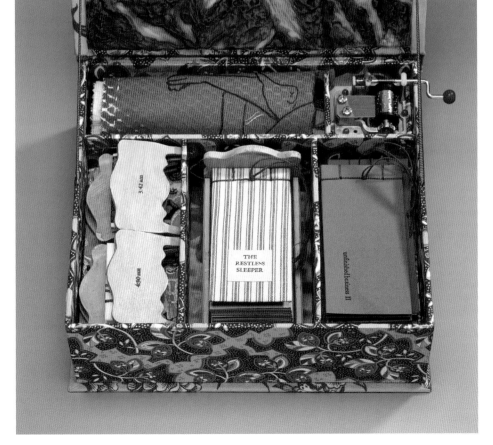

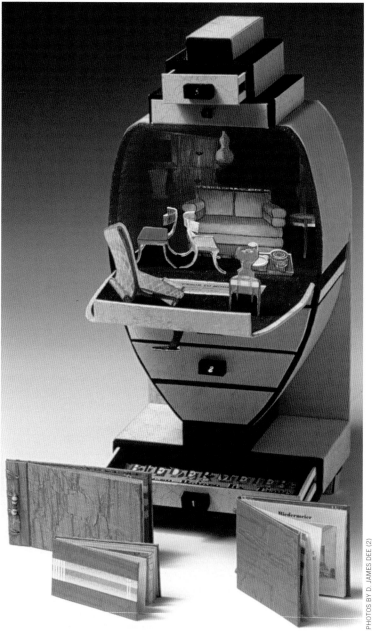

0715, 0716
Laurie Spitz, Amee Pollack, Spitz & Pollack, USA

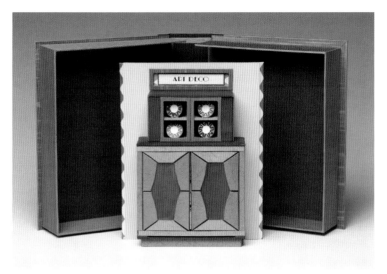
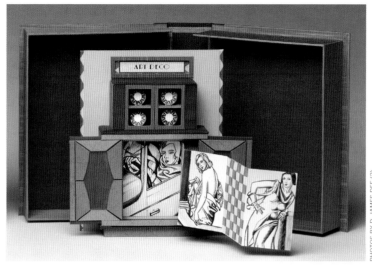

0717, 0718
Laurie Spitz, Amee Pollack, Spitz & Pollack, USA

0719, 0720, 0721
Lawrence G. Van Veleer, Peggy Gotthold,
Foolscap Press, USA

0722, 0723, 0724
Susan Collard, USA

0725, 0726
Susan Collard, USA

0727
Daniel Essig, USA

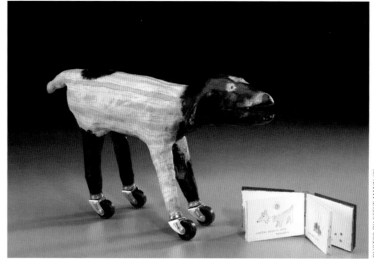

PHOTOS BY STEVE MANN (2)

0728, 0729
Margaret Couch Cogswell, USA

PHOTO BY STEVE MANN

0730
Margaret Couch Cogswell, USA

0731
Libby Barrett, USA

[0732
Mia Leijonstedt, UK

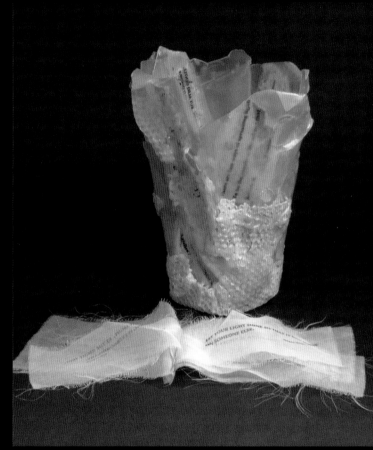

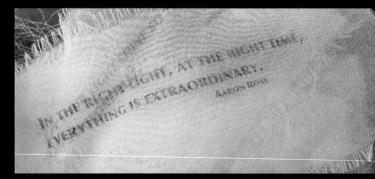

[0733, 0734
Josie Rodriguez, USA

0735
Marlis Maehrle, GERMANY

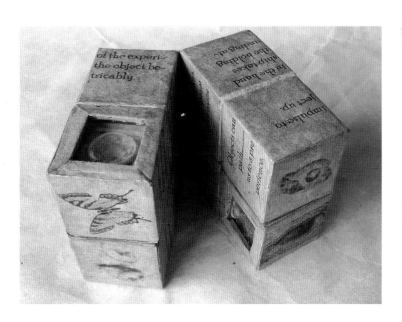

0736
Sandy Webster, USA

0737, 0738
Jan Sobota,
CZECH REPUBLIC

all i have
to give you
is my weakness

you have lost the power
of astonishment
at your own actions

PHOTO BY COREY HOCHACHKA, TROGLODYTE PHOTOGRAPHY

0739, 0740, 0741
Edward van Vliet, CANADA

0742
Suzanne Reese
Horvitz, USA

0743, 0744, 0745
Robert Roesch, USA

0746, 0747
Marie Marcano, USA

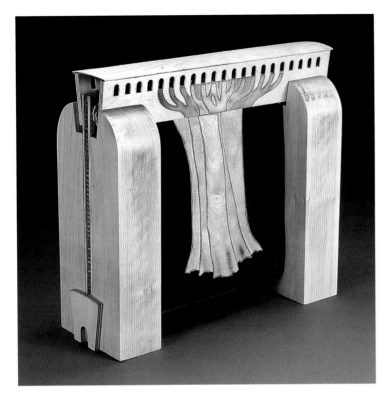

0748, 0749
Dolph Smith, USA

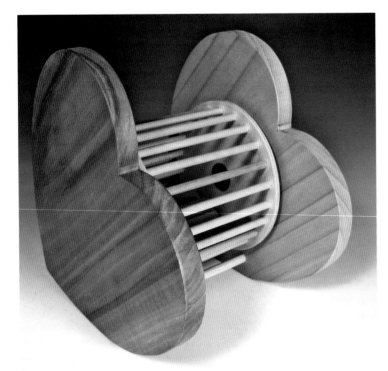

0750, 0751
Dolph Smith, USA

PHOTO BY BUKVA IMAGING GROUP

0752
Eugenie Torgerson, USA

0753, 0754
Benjamin D. Rinehart, USA

Pamela Paulsrud, USA

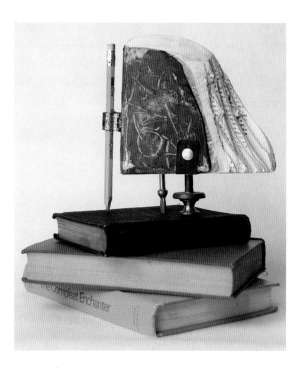

0756
Pamela Paulsrud, USA

0757
Randi Parkhurst, USA

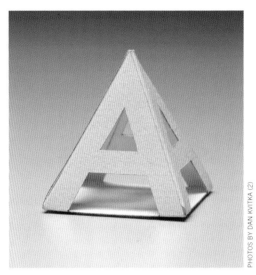

PHOTOS BY DAN KVITKA (2)

0758, 0759
Helen Hiebert, Helen Hiebert Studio, USA

PHOTO BY LIA ROOSENDAAL, JAGWIRE DESIGN

0760
Lisa Kokin, USA

0761, 0762
Irina Yablochkina, RUSSIA

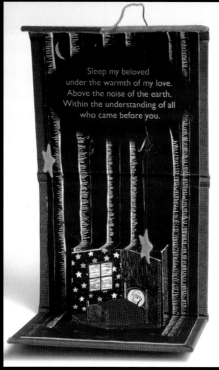

Sleep my beloved
under the warmth of my love.
Above the noise of the earth.
Within the understanding of all
who came before you.

0764
Camille Riner, USA

0763
Irina Yablochkina, RUSSIA

0765, 0766
Sandra C. Fernandez,
USA

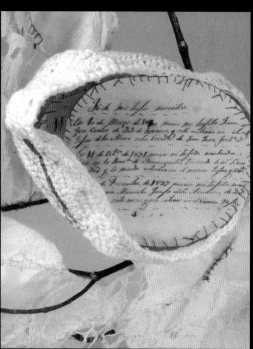

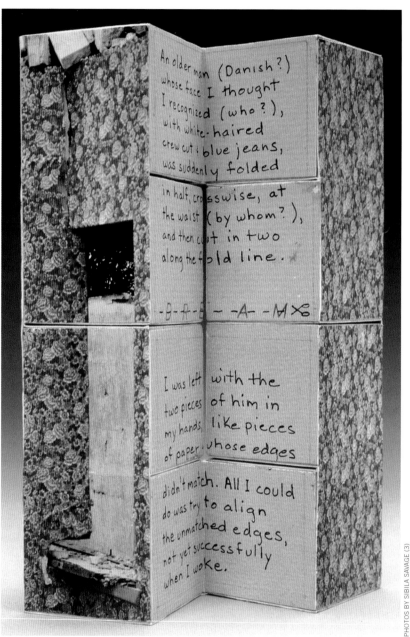

An older man (Danish?) whose face I thought I recognized (who?), with white-haired crew cut & blue jeans, was suddenly folded in half, crosswise, at the waist (by whom?), and then cut in two along the fold line.

-B-A-B- -A- -MX6

I was left with the two pieces of him in my hands, like pieces of paper whose edges didn't match. All I could do was try to align the unmatched edges, not yet successfully when I woke.

0767, 0768, 0769
Betsy Davids, USA

0770
Ellen Gradman, USA

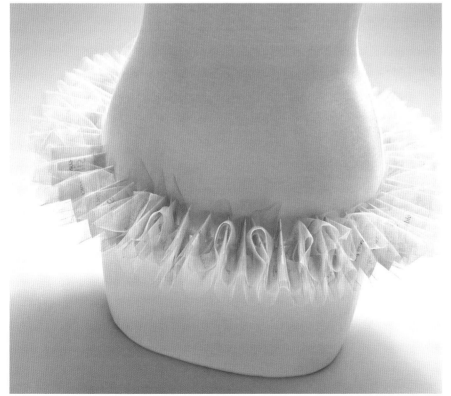

0771, 0772
Kelly O'Brien,
TurningPointe Press, GERMANY

[0773
Irmari Nacht, USA

[0774, 0775
Annell Livingston,
USA

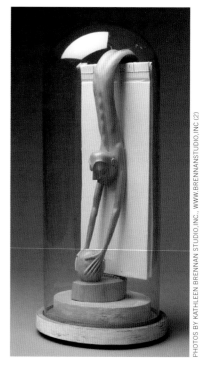

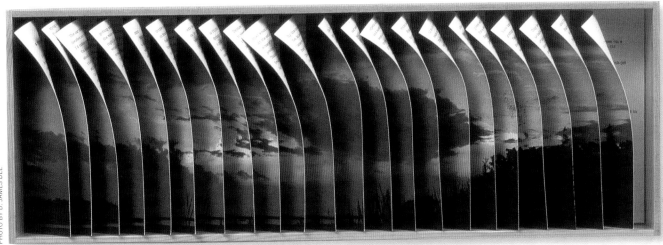

0776
Katherine D. Crone,
USA

0777, 0778
Annell Livingston,
USA

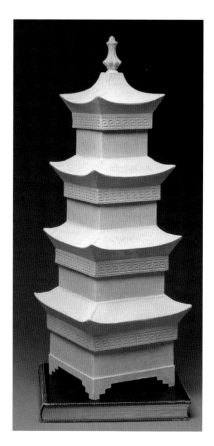

PHOTOS BY KATHLEEN BRENNAN STUDIO,INC., WWW.BRENNANSTUDIO,INC (2)

[0779, 0780
Annell Livingston, USA

[0781, 0782
Ania Gilmore and
Annie Zeybekoglu, USA

0783, 0784

Kelly O'Brien, TurningPointe Press, GERMANY

PHOTOS BY JIM VECCHIONE (2)

0785, 0786

Sandra T. Donabed,
Ganymede Studio, USA

0787
Erin Sweeney,
Lovely In The Home Press, USA

0788, 0789
Diane Jacobs,
Scantron Press, USA

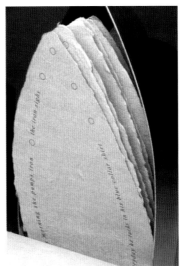

0790, 0791
Kerri Cushman,
performing goats press, USA

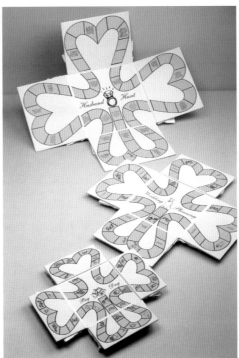

0792, 0793, 0794
Jen Thomas, Veronica Press, USA

0795
Brian Dettmer, USA

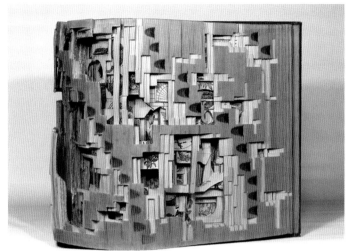

0796, 0797
Brian Dettmer, USA

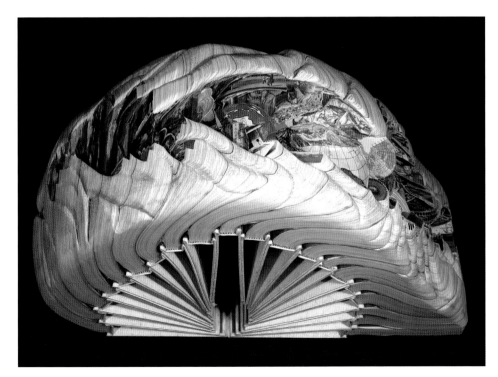

0798, 0799
Brian Dettmer, USA

PHOTO BY CHELSEA ODUM

0800
Lynn Sures, USA

0801, 0802
Eugenie Torgerson,
USA

0803

Sarah Bodman, Bookarts at
the Centre for Fine Print
Research, UK

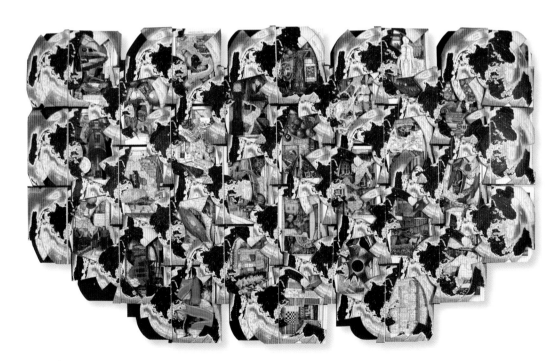

0804, 0805

Brian Dettmer, USA

0806, 0807
Marcia Weisbrot, Pencilhead Press, USA

0808, 0809, 0810
Lisa Hasegawa, ilfant press, USA

0811, 0812
Shawn Kathleen Simmons, USA

0813, 0814
Sue Huggins Leopard,
Leopard Studio Editions, USA

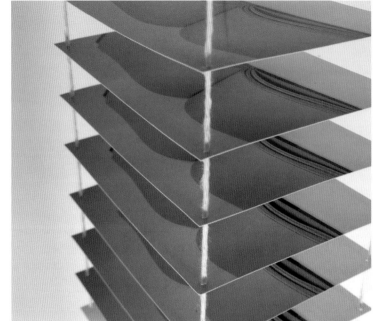

0815, 0816
Dennis Yuen, USA

0817
Viviana Lombrozo, USA

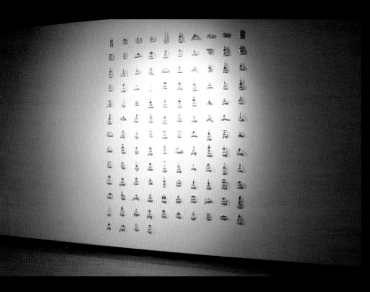

0818, 0819
Susan Porteous,
USA

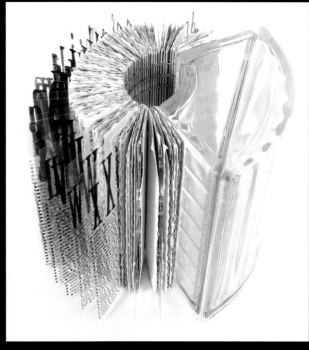

0820, 0821
Jill Pollock, USA

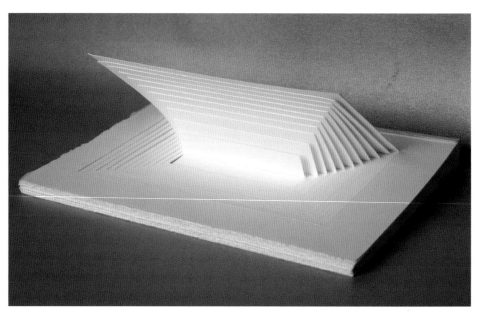

0823
Regula Russelle, USA

0822
Marilyn R. Rosenberg, USA

0824
Adèle Outteridge, Studio West
End, AUSTRALIA

PHOTO BY ALENKA SLAVINEC

0825
Béatrice Coron, USA

0826, 0827
Shu-Ju Wang, USA

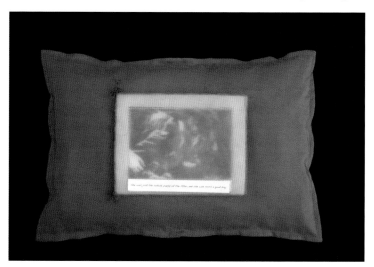
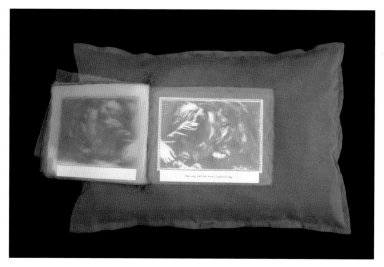

[0828, 0829, 0830
[**Daniel E. Kelm, Wide Awake Garage,** USA

[0831
  Leslie M. Madigan,
  USA

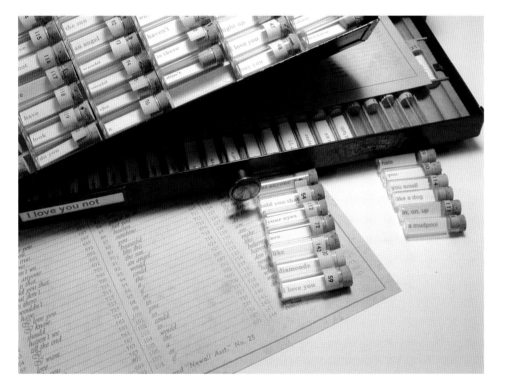

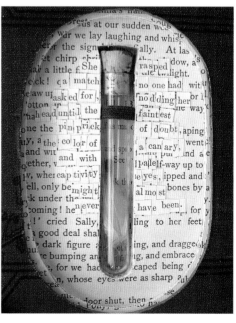

0832, 0833
Merike van Zanten,
Double Dutch Design, USA

0834, 0835
Brooke Schmidt, USA

0836
Katherine D. Crone, USA

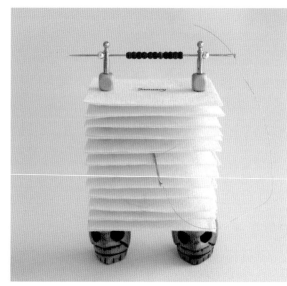

0837
Heather Crossley,
AUSTRALIA

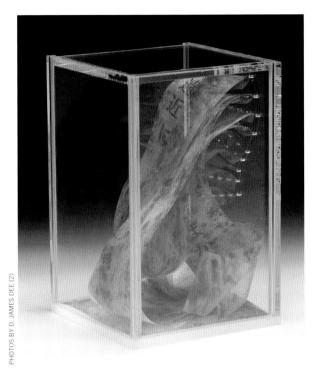

0838, 0839

Katherine D. Crone,
USA

0840, 0841

Robbin Ami Silverberg, Dobbin Mill/Dobbin Books, USA

0842, 0843, 0844
Jill K. Berry, USA

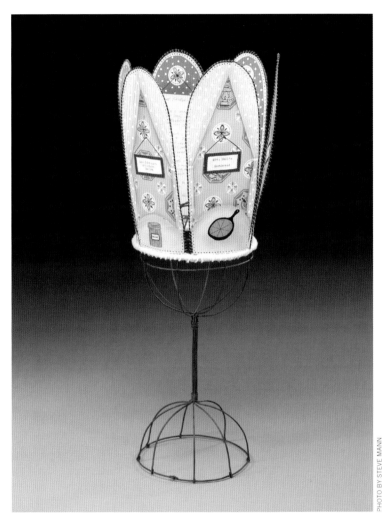

0845
Margaret Couch Cogswell, USA

0846
Margaret Couch Cogswell, USA

0847, 0848
Guy Laramée, CANADA

0849
Guy Laramée, CANADA

0850
Guy Laramée, CANADA

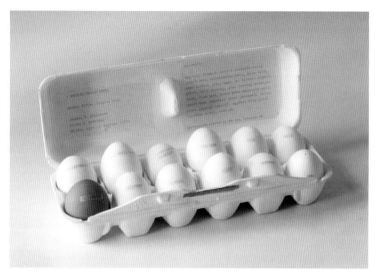

PHOTOS BY ERIC BLUM (2)

0851, 0852

Alaska McFadden & Jessica Elsaesser,
A Wrecked Tangle Press, USA

0853, 0854

Lynne Kelly, USA

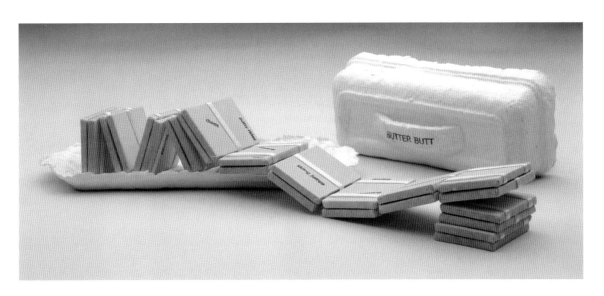

0855

Kerri Cushman, performing goats press, USA

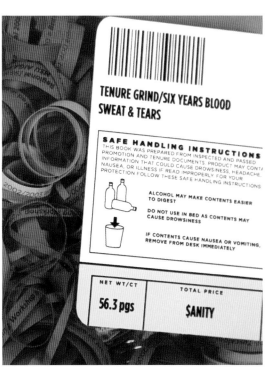

0856, 0857

Jamie Runnells, Jamie Runnells Designs, USA

[0858, 0859
Doug Beube, USA

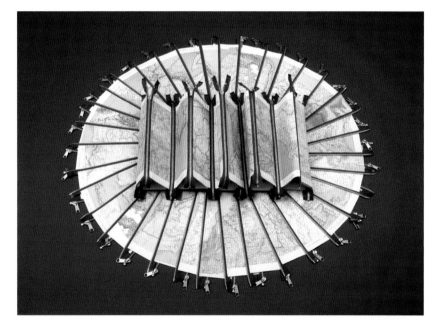

[0860, 0861
Doug Beube, USA

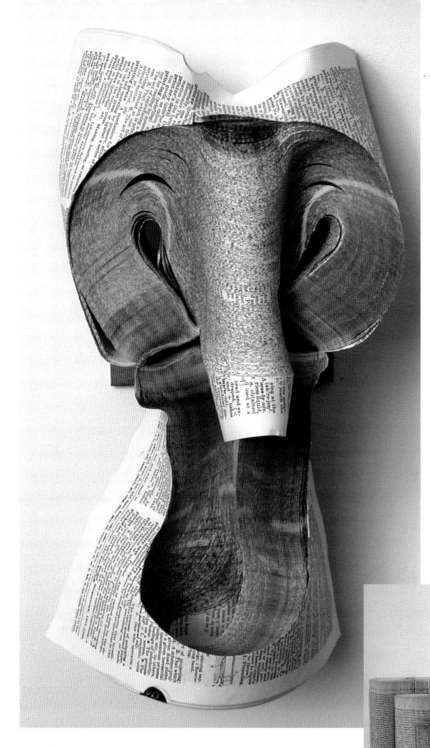

0863
Doug Beube, USA

0862
Doug Beube, USA

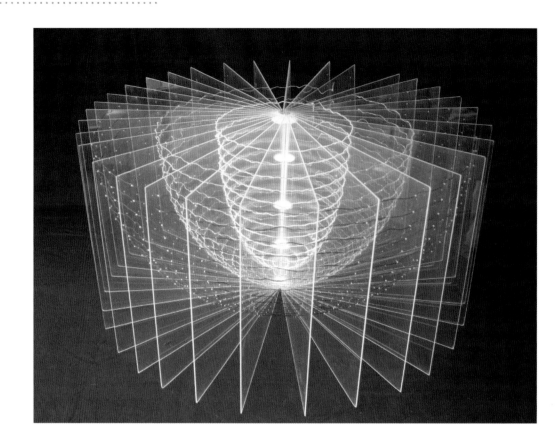

0864
Adèle Outteridge,
Studio West End,
AUSTRALIA

0865, 0866
Jarmila Jelena Sobotova, CZECH REPUBLIC

0868
Author Roberta Lavadour, Mission Creek Press, USA

0867
Adèle Outteridge, Wim de Vos,
Studio West End, AUSTRALIA

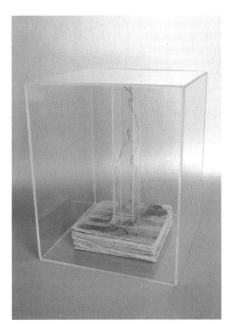

0869, 0870
Adèle Outteridge,
Studio West End, AUSTRALIA

0871
Barbara Bussolari, USA

Why are we
More curious
About the
Meaning of
Dreams

Than about
What we
See when
We are
Awake.

Barbara Bussolari

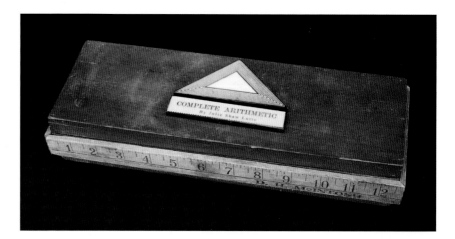

0872, 0873
Julie Shaw Lutts, USA

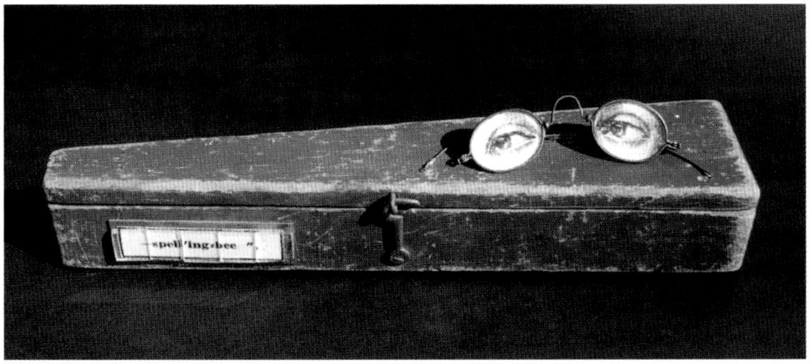

0874, 0875, 0876
Julie Shaw Lutts, USA

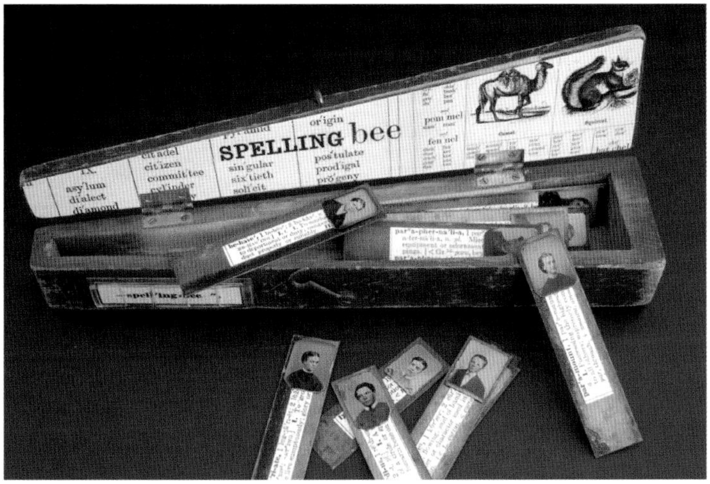

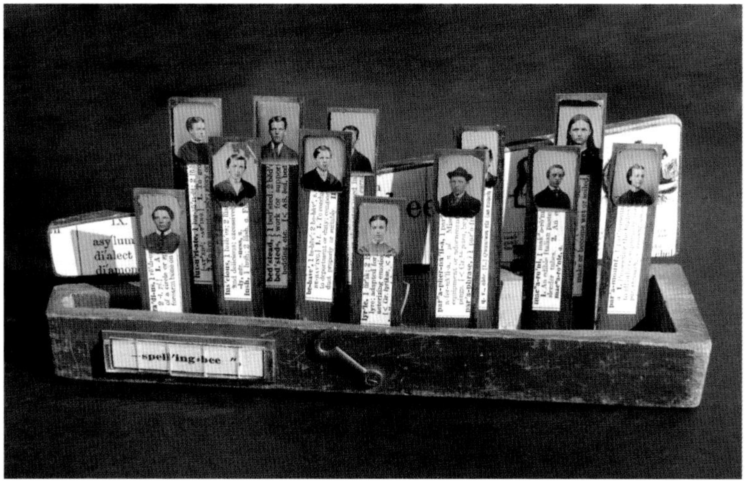

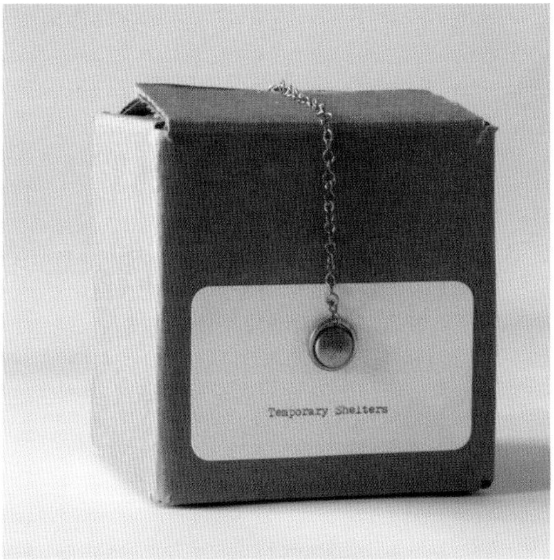

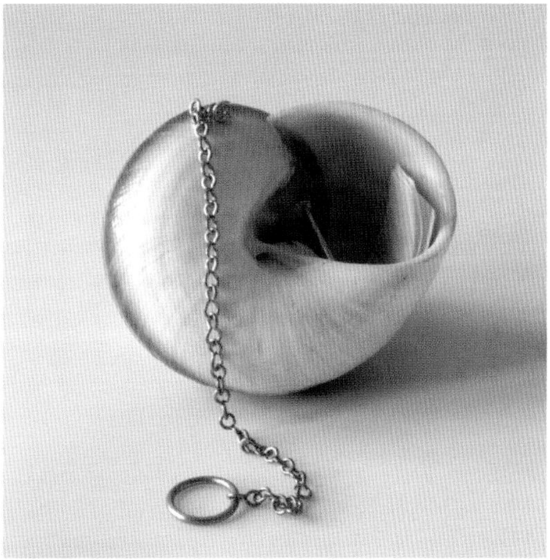

0877, 0878
Alaska McFadden &
Jessica Elsaesser,
A Wrecked Tangle Press, USA

PHOTOS BY ERIC BLUM (2)

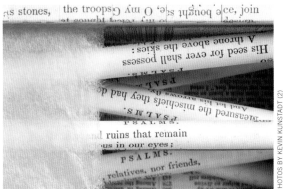

0879, 0880
Carole P. Kunstadt, USA

0881
Eleonora Cumer,
ITALY

PHOTO BY KEVIN KUNSTADT

0882
Carole P. Kunstadt, USA

0883
Sandy Webster, USA

0884, 0885
Irmari Nacht, USA

0886, 0887
Catherine Nash, USA

0888, 0889
Gail Stiffe, Hands on Paper,
AUSTRALIA

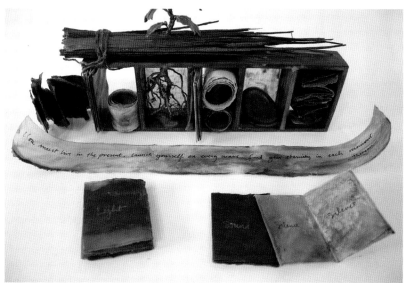

0892
Peggy Johnston,
Waveland Studio, USA

0890, 0891
Catherine Nash, USA

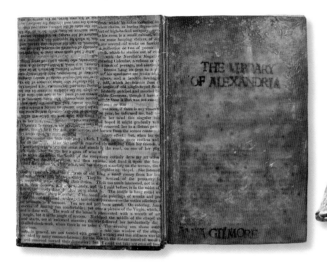

0893, 0894
Ania Gilmore, USA

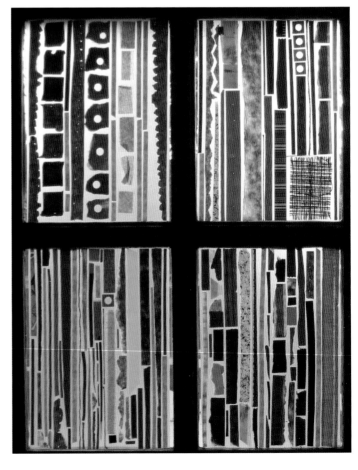

0895, 0896
Peter Madden, USA

0897, 0898
Tom Virgin, USA

0899, 0900
Sun Young Kang, USA

0901, 0902
Dorit Elisha, USA

0903, 0904
Richard Kegler,
USA

0905, 0906

Merike van Zanten,
Double Dutch Design, USA

PHOTO BY TULLIS JOHNSON

0907

Richard Kegler, USA

0908

Isabelle Faivre, FRANCE

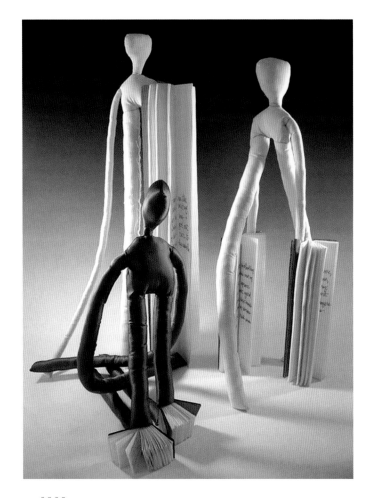

0909
Erin Sweeney,
Lovely In The Home Press, USA

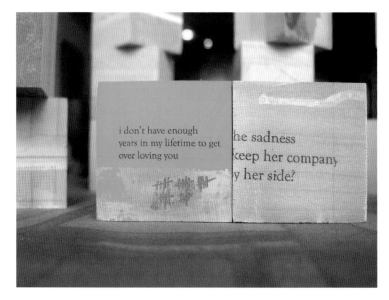

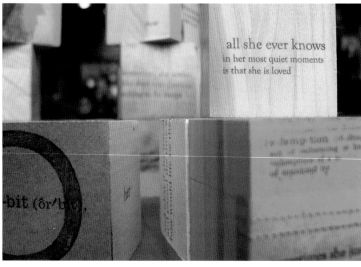

0910, 0911
e Bond,
roughdrAft books,
USA

0912, 0913
Bessie Smith Moulton, USA

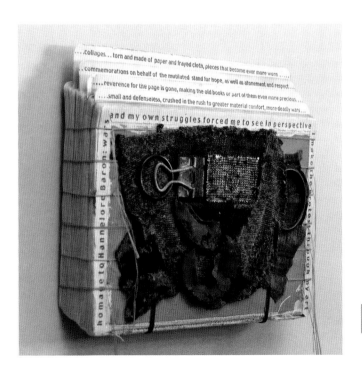

0915
Helen Sanderson,
AUSTRALIA

0914
Genie Shenk, USA

[0916
Jarmila Jelena Sobotova,
CZECH REPUBLIC

PHOTO BY STEPHEN DESANTIS

[0917
Miriam Schaer, USA

[0918
Miriam Schaer, USA

[0919
Hilke Kurzke, Büchertiger Studio
& Press, GERMANY

0920, 0921

Erica Spitzer Rasmussen, USA

0922

Erica Spitzer Rasmussen,
USA

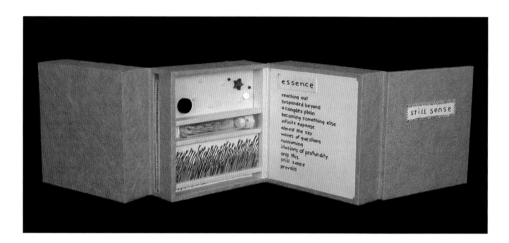

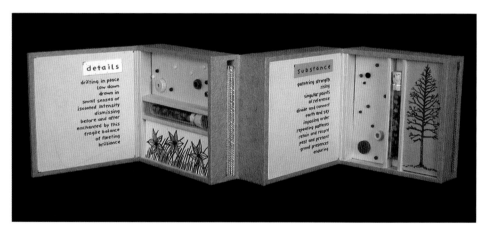

0923, 0924
Jody Williams,
Flying Paper Press, USA

0925
Anne C. Gable, USA

0926
Antonio Claudio Carvalho,
BRAZIL

0927, 0928
Melissa Jay Craig, USA

0929
Lisa Kokin, USA

0930, 0931

Bonnie Thompson
Norman,
The Windowpane
Press, USA

0932

Meda R. Rives,
Veda M. Rives,
Mirror Image Press, USA

PHOTOS BY BETH FORMAN (2)

0933, 0934
Purgatory Pie Press, Dikko Faust + Esther K Smith,
collaborating artist: Michael Bartalos, USA

0935
Kumi Korf, USA

0936
Viviana
Lombrozo,
USA

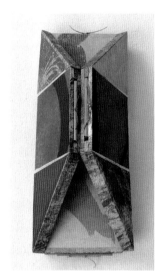

0937, 0938, 0939
Kumi Korf, USA

0940, 0941
Ke Francis, Hoopsnake Press,
USA

0942, 0943
Earle D. Swope, USA

0944, 0945
Marilyn R. Rosenberg, USA

[0946
Rachael Ashe, CANADA

PHOTO BY JOHN POLAK PHOTOGRAPHY

[0947
Sharon McCartney, USA

[0948, 0949
Cathy DeForest,
Jubilation Press, USA

0950, 0951, 0952
Tom Virgin, USA

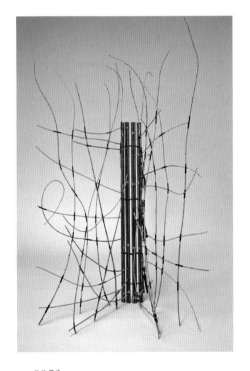

0954
Sharon
Armstead,
AUSTRALIA

0953
Lark Burkhart,
Jumping Crow Studio, USA

0955, 0956
Melissa Jay Craig, USA

0957
Rachelle W. Chuang,
Rachelle W. Chuang Art & Design, USA

0958
Lark Burkhart,
Jumping Crow Studio, USA

0959, 0960, 0961
Ke Francis,
Hoopsnake Press, USA

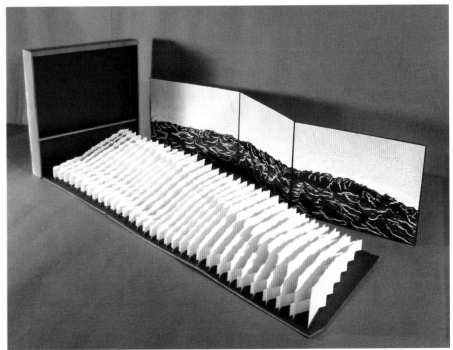

0962, 0963, 0964
Thomas Parker Williams, USA

0965, 0966
Sammy Lee,
Studio SML/K, USA

0967
Kestutis Vasiliunas,
LITHUANIA

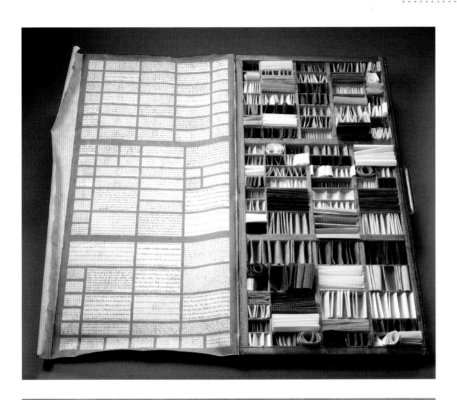

I can't take it anymore! People are always calling me crazy!

I used to be steadfast, trustworthy, accomplished. The 3's looked up to me like a parent. Then somehow I end up watching the Olympics with 6, and it's all over. I should have tried swimming, but those Russian girls were just so fetching.

When people say "It's all for naught," I feel the weight of the world on my shoulders.

So I'm the sar such a limiting *M*, she unders your full-figur

As the resident lucky number of most everyone in town, I get summoned often. Mostly it's the gamblers; I really shouldn't identify them though.

fi and I learned a long time ago that we can pass ourselves off as non-ligatures to the untrained eye. While *ffi*, *ffl*, and *ff* revel in their ligature-ness, we are a little more practical. We have to be. I mean, they all live on the outskirts of town where it's OK to be eccentric. *fi* and I are squeezed in between the numbers and the lower case mob. We don't want to draw attention.

ff is like a brother to me; I pretty much follow his lead. But the truth is, he'll never feel the pain of loss that I do. He's not missing a thing. Two *f*'s, big deal. Meanwhile, I lost the dot to my *i*. Sometimes it's like a phantom limb; I almost think I can still feel it there, in all its perfect roundness. *ff* is all about passing as non-ligs; me, I'm still in mourning for *i*.

I am so tired of hearir existence, but that's C of you is needed! Ol

When *9* took up gymnastics, he started with a forward roll, and ended up as me. Incredibly, no one has ever noticed that we never appear in the same room at the same time.

In physics I stand for gravity. Pretty important, right? And yet here I am stuck between *f* and his imitators. What a lightweight *f* is. And *ff* and *fi* are so deluded; they think no one notices them as imagination-less ligatures. How did I ever get stuck here? You cannot have a gerund without me! Drop me and you sound like so uneducated.

I feel like finished, es but don't g me off, and

Number of fingers on one hand?

Number of toes on one foot?

Coincidence? I think not.

I have a lot of imitators. The ligatures follow my every move, obviously. But did you know about my deep connection to *v*? We sound so much alike, that she helps me out when I venture into the plural - like wives, knives, thieves. She's a peach. I do like to have fun, that is true, and I pretty much hang with *n* most of the time. But we are both pestered by *i*. She is constantly pressing up against us to spell *if* and *in* when we are just trying to have a little *fun* with *u*. Sometimes I have to use my f-word with her. I tell her to go make *it* with *t*.

Most people don't for *qu*. Since they of that Internet th name, it's amazing

[0968, 0969
Donna Globus, USA

[0970
Tracie Morris Easler, USA

0972
Suzanne Reese Horvitz,
USA

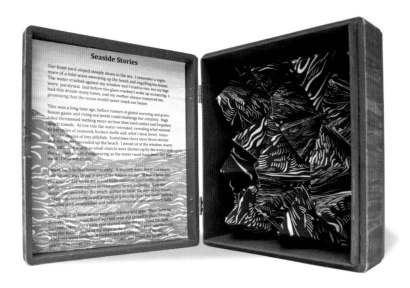

0971
Barbara Milman,
Red Parrot Press, USA

0973
Regula Russelle, USA

0974, 0975
Karen Hanmer, USA

0976
Art Hazelwood,
USA

0977
Leslie M. Madigan,
USA

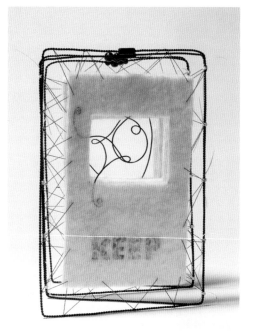

0978, 0979
Robyn A. Daniel, USA

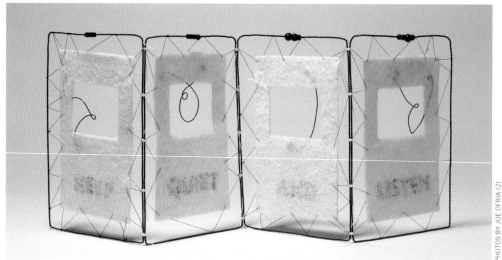

PHOTO BY MARK GULEZIAN, QUICKSILVER

0980
Lynn Sures, USA

0981
Lisa Avramidou, Schema Books, UK

0982, 0983
**Meghan Hawkes, Meghan Hawkes
Photography & Bookarts,** USA

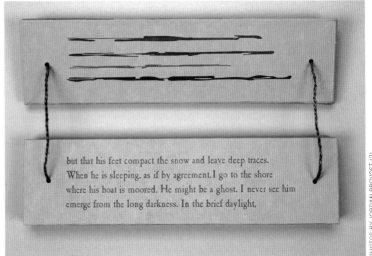

[0984, 0985
Roni Gross, Z'roah Press, USA

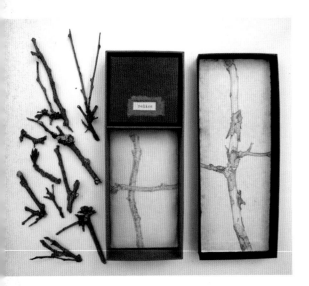

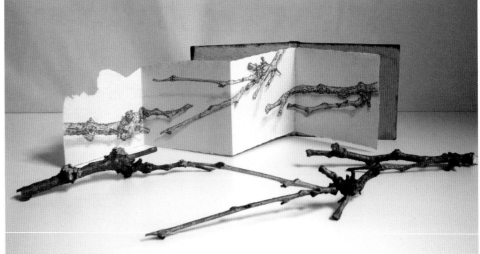

[0986, 0987
Suzanne Barnes, USA

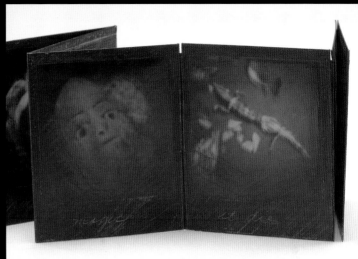

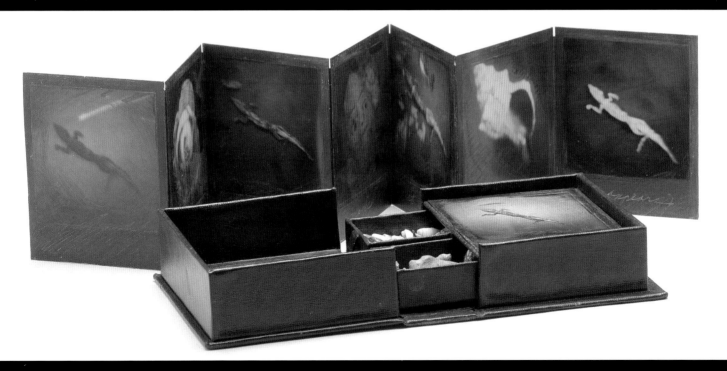

0988, 0989, 0990
Judith Golden, USA

0991, 0992
Carol Norby, USA

0993
Carolyn Shattuck, Shattuck Studio & Gallery, USA

0994, 0995
Jessica Spring, Springtide Press, USA

0996, 0997
Daniel E. Kelm,
Wide Awake Garage, USA

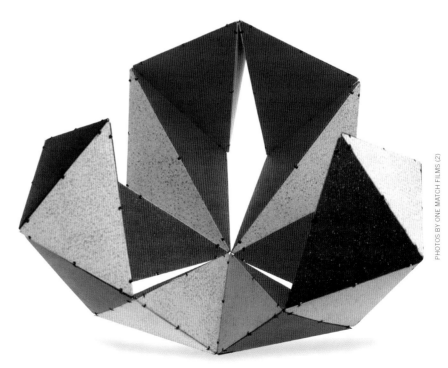

0998
Daniel Essig, USA

0999, 1000
Richard Minsky, USA

Image Directory

0001 Chained Album (6 x 4 x 3 in [15.0 x 10.0 x 7.5 cm]): Ethiopian and Coptic bindings with mahogany and ebony woods, mica, fossil, tintypes, and handmade paper.

0002, 0003, 0004 Altered (3 x 2½ x 2 in [7.5 x 6.3 x 5.0 cm]): Ethiopian and Coptic bindings with walnut, mica, fossils, shell, and handmade Cave paper. Wire-wrapped stone by Bob Ebendorf.

0005, 0006 See Through (5 x 5 x 2⅛ in [12.5 x 12.5 x 5.3 cm]): Coptic bound book with a window in the cover made with Lenox paper, bookcloth, glass microscope slides, alstromeria petal, mull, waxed linen thread, and Davey board. Interior created with acrylic ink and gesso painted papers, original handwritten text, cutouts, and pop-up pages.

0007, 0008 Drawing Dragons (4½ x 6 x 2 in [11.3 x 15.0 x 5.0 cm]): Original illustrations and text with binder's own oak gall ink, carved wood cover, and nonadhesive coptic stitch.

0009, 0010 In My Grandmothers' Gardens (5 x 3½ x 2 in [12.5 x 8.8 x 5.0 cm]): Distressed milk-painted wooden covers, coptic binding, and mica pages with original collages and handwritten text hinged with stained Tyvek; leather strap with bone closure.

0011, 0012 Fragments (4½ x 4½ in [11.3 x 11.3 cm]): Original collages including transfer prints, pochoir, gelatin prints, stitching, and acetate on handmade paper. Coptic binding by Crystal Cawley.

0013 Temptation (5 x 4 x 3 in [12.5 x 10.0 x 7.5 cm]): Hand-carved basswood painted with milk paint. Coptic stitching, handmade end papers.

0014, 0015 The Bird's Book (5 x 3½ x 1½ in [12.5 x 8.8 x 3.8 cm]): Wooden covers with birch bark laminate and a mica window containing a clay egg. Interior pages of Somerset and vellum with pochoir, original watercolors and gouache, and letterpress printing. Coptic binding by Crystal Cawley.

0016, 0017, 0018 Book of Trees (2½ x 2 x 2½ in [6.3 x 5.0 x 6.3 cm]): Artists' calligraphy on Japanese paper of a fourteenth century Welsh legend translated by Robert Graves, separated with wooden leaves. Nonadhesive coptic stitch with leather and bark cover.

0019 Small Universe (4 x 3 x 2½ in [10.0 x 7.5 x 6.3 cm]): Fourth century Coptic-style binding, using hand-carved linden wood, milk paint, India Ink, and the artist's handmade paper.

0020, 0021 Dreams 2005: I Went to Sleep, Where Did I Go? (4 x 4 x 1½ in [10.0 x 10.0 x 3.8 cm]): A daily dream record with original handwritten and collaged text and artwork utilizing image transfers and ink on Cave paper and board. Coptic binding.

0022, 0023 The Bears Book (10 x 2 ½ x 7 ¼ in [25.0 x 6.3 x 18.1 cm]): Coptic-bound book of original mixed media illustrations with gold leaf, original inkjet-printed text, and original calligraphy on Thai Mulberry and Japanese papers and Alabaster translucent papers.

Reliquary box of acid-free paperboard, ultrasuede, and leather with acrylic and India ink.

0024, 0025, 0026 Curiosities (3½ x 3 1/8 x 1⅛ in [8.8 x 7.8 x 2.8 cm]): Original monotypes on Rives BFK, with an exposed-sewn binding with coptic stitching. Book housed in a hand-built stained and glazed porcelain box along with porcelain reproductive organs.

0027, 0028, 0029 To Please My Fancy (5 x 5 x 3 in [12.5 x 12.5 x 7.5 cm]): Text by unknown author hand-embroidered onto handkerchiefs screenprinted with original illustrations. Screenprinted binder's board cover, coptic binding.

0030, 0031 zero to twelve (4 x 2½ x 3½ in [10.0 x 6.3 x 8.8 cm]): Single sheet coptic binding with waxed cotton cord. Transparent plexiglass lightly sanded with used sandpaper to make it translucent. The numbers cut from copper, and objects attached with rivets, tiny nuts and bolts, and liquid nails.

0032, 0033 Simple Pleasures (9 x 12 x ½ in [22.5 x 30 x 1.3 cm]): Original color etching and embossing on Fabriano Murillo, drawing and handwritten text on Sekishu Japanese paper, with mylar cover. Coptic binding with chain stitched spine.

0034, 0035, 0036 The CORE of James Farmer (8½ x 6⅜ x ½ in [21.3 x 15.9 x 1.3 cm]): Letterpress-printed text by Detine L. Bowers with an embroidered davy board cover; coptic binding.

0037, 0038 Travel Log: My Travels in China (8½ x 5½ x 2½ in [21.3 x 13.8 x 6.3 cm]): Cover made from reconstructed vintage Chinese waste basket, artist-made figures with beards of real hair, leather spine, and long-stitch binding. Original calligraphy and painting, interior text by Wendy L. Smith.

0039, 0040, 0041 Lines (8½ x 7½ x ½ in [21.3 x 18.8 x 1.3 cm]): Newspaper images painted with lines, and silk stitched with lines. Coptic binding and a clamshell box made by John DeMerritt.

0042, 0043 Wabi Sabi Elements, Wabi Sabi Words (4 x 3 x 3 in [10.0 x 7.5 x 7.5 cm]): Evoking the Japanese Wabi Sabi aesthetic through inkjet text, Asian paper, and found metal elements.

0044, 0045 Fem (9½ x 8¾ x 1¼ in [23.8 x 21.9 x 3.1 cm]): Original poetry accompanied by found vintage photos and original illustrations and collage on handmade papers by Ann Silverman; cover of natural light canvas with satin wrap closure. Coptic binding.

0046 stick with love (6 x 6 in [15.0 x 15.0 cm]): Original drawings printed on Japanese paper and a quote by Martin Luther King Jr., with hand-sewn caterpillar binding.

0047, 0048 Feedmee Chocol8 Mousse (2 x 3½ x 1¼ in [5.0 x 8.8 x 3.1 cm]): Beeswax coated prints and nonsensical text, bound with a caterpillar stitch.

0049, 0050, 0051 Unearthed (8 x 4 in [20.0 x 10.0 cm]): Hand-made, hand-shaped abaca paper cover, interior of hand-cut paper with original lithography printing. Reverse Turkish map fold, pamphlet stitch.

0052, 0053 Wild Girls Redux: An Operator's Manual (9 x 5 x ½ in [22.5 x 12.5 x 1.3 cm]): Comparing driving rules with the unspoken rules society imposes on women. Accordion fold structure with pamphlet stitch incorporating original text and illlustrations letterpress printed from photopolymer plates onto a mix of papers and doilies, flocked paper, and Hahnemühle Bugra. Cover of Indian Sun Hemp Contemporary paper.

0054, 0055 The Whole Is Greater Than the Sum of Its Parts (12¼ x 9¾ x 1¾ in [30.6 x 24.4 x 4.4 cm]): Five interlocking single-sheet pamphlet stitched books with original text and illustrations in pencil and acetone transfer on paper, housed in a book board case.

0056, 0057 Paszport (5¼ x 4 x ¼ in [13.1 x 10.0 x 0.6 cm]): Single signature pamphlet of archival inkjet prints of digitally designed collages about immigration from Poland to the USA.

0058, 0059 Box of Growth (6¾ x 3¼ x 2¼ in [16.9 x 8.1 x 5.6 cm]): Five pamphlet-stitched accordion books in a handmade paper slipcase. Original math drawings, hand-set type and letterpress printing. Assorted handmade papers for covers and endsheets, Johannot interior papers.

0060, 0061, 0062 The Short Goodbye (12¼ x 8½ x ¼ in [30.6 x 21.3 x 0.6 cm]): Quotes from Raymond Chandler's *The Long Goodbye* formatted into thematic typographic shapes. Hand-set letterpress type. Covers of metallic black and silver Indian paper over boards, shot with a 9 mm pistol. Seven of the editions are housed in a louvered wooden box.

0063 Ukulele Series Book #14, Old Ukes (18 x 12 x 7 in [45.0 x 30.0 x 17.5 cm]): Covers are playable ukuleles. Pages are old ukulele tops, attached to the spine with brass hinges (no good uke was harmed in the creation of this artwork).

0064, 0065, 0066 Rondo (16¾ x 11¾ x ½ in [41.9 x 29.4 x 1.3 cm]): Artist's interpretation of Istvan Örkény's novella. Nontraditional folded structure and codex triptych, with cover of Dobbin Mill papers and silk book cloth with embedded DVD. Archival inkjet printing and manual typewriter text on Dobbin Mill papers, pulp painting. DVD of sound performance included.

0067, 0068, 0069 Solomon's Wisdom: A Fable A Poem A Eulogy A Dream Ten Nests and Eight Holes (13 x 12 x 1½ in [32.5 x 30.0 x 3.8 cm]): Three original texts plus fragments of Pablo Neruda's poem, "The Word," archival inkjet printed with original photographs on Dobbin Mill papers. Ripped, re-stapled, and filigree-cut pages with pulp painting. Cover of Dobbin Mill papers and silk book cloth. Illustrates that the sum cannot equal the whole.

0070, 0071, 0072, 0073 Panorama (9½ x 20¼ x 1¼ in [23.8 x 50.6 x 3.1 cm]): Original text and artwork, letterpress printed on a variety of papers using photopolymer plates and wood blocks, with large format pop-ups and interactive folded sections. This book explores the issue of climate change. Case-bound codex format using adhesive; opens to five feet (1.5 m).

0074, 0075 **Pyramid, New York** (27 x 20 x 3½ in [67.5 x 50.0 x 8.8 cm]): Wood covers with etched and colored brass. Brown paper bag pages with original Xerox transfers, stitching, and laser printing. Modified Japanese side-sewn binding.

0076, 0077 **Mullings** (15 x 11 x 3½ in [37.5 x 27.5 x 8.8 cm]): One-hundred-sixty paintings in ink, watercolor, graphite, and acrylics on paper. Iron, gold, and sand on paper covered boards and leather on the binding. Sewn binding with single coil endbands, waxed dry pigment edges.

0078, 0079, 0080 **The Pencil** (8 ½ x 5 ½ x 1 in [21.3 x 13.8 x 2.5]): Tri-fold binding, leather and letterpress printed handmade paper made from cedar wood pulp with vintage pencils in pencil cedar holder. Text is an original history of the pencil, handwritten in pencil, reproduced by color laser printing. Housed in a cedar "pencil" box with pencils at the foredge.

0081 **Bad Girls** (8½ x 6 x 1¼ in [21.3 x 15.0 x 3.1 cm]): Set of six dos-à-dos books. Layered paper covers with acrylic and original paper collages interiors.

0082, 0083 **Once Westinghouse** (12 x 19 x 2 in [30.0 x 47.5 x 5.0 cm]): Digital reproductions and pen and ink artwork with a cover of handmade abaca, cast abaca, wood, and plastic.

0084, 0085 **Actias Luna** (6 x 7 x 1½ in [15.0 x 17.5 x 3.8 cm]): Original poem about an encounter with two lunas, ink over gouache on daylily papers, with beaded moth on leather. Case paper stationer's binding, tacketed, with hand-built paper button closure.

0086, 0087, 0088 **There Be Monsters** (5½ x 5⅜ x ⅜ in [13.8 x 13.4 x 0.9 cm]): Original story and artwork. Sewn onto straps laced through folded Iowa PC4 G paper, copper foil stamped title. Printed via letterpress in 12 and 18 point Lutetia with a hand-colored wood engraving and a 6 color linoleum cut.

0089, 0090 **Myeongwol / bright moon talisman** (2 x 2¼ x 1¼ in [5.0 x 5.6 x 3.1 cm]): Inkjet prints of an original poem about Hwang Jin-i, a sixteenth century Korean gisaeng, on hanji (Korean handmade paper), sewn onto pages of knitted pine paper yarn, with an original binding made of naturally-dyed and woven hanji.

0091, 0092 **Nobody Gets A Free Ride** (13 x 3 x 2½ in [32.5 x 7.5 x 6.3 cm]): Original block printed illustrations on blueprints, aluminum screening, with covers of recycled shingle slats. Coptic and long-stitch bindings.

0093, 0094 **Meter** (9 x 6 x 1 in [22.5 x 15.0 x 2.5 cm]): Original text and illustrations inkjet printed and laser cut on Somerset paper and plastic. Cover of Asahi bookcloth, Moriki paper, leather, and linen waxed thread.

0095, 0096, 0097 **Oh Come Let Us Adore Him** (12 x 9½ x 4 in [30.0 x 23.8 x 10.0 cm]): Xerox transfer of original text and illustrations, with added hand-stitching on paper and cotton. Found wood covers with paper and cotton pages. Modified Japanese side-sewn binding.

0098 **Fountains Abbey** (7¼ x 5⅛ x ⅞ in [18.1 x 12.8 x 2.2 cm]): Original watercolor fore-edge painting.

0099, 0100 **The Seven Stages of Women (with Apologies to William Shakespeare)** (9¾ x 5 ⅞ x 2¼ in [24.4 x 14.7 x 5.6 cm]): Cover made from handmade paper by Katie MacGregor over boards aged with pigment and wax, and a Cave Paper spine. The interior contains

dimensional objects including brass number stencils, unexposed glass negatives, and locks and keys. The book is wrapped in a vintage linen napkin, tied with a tea-dyed trim, and housed in a vintage silk box.

0101, 0102 **Hip Hop at Fifteen** (2 x 5¾ x ½ in [5 x 14.4 x 1.3 cm]): Photographic flipbook printed on semi-gloss double-sided photographic paper, with lyrics from the chorus of "The Craft" by Blackalicious.

0103, 0104, 0105 **In Quest of Treasure** (6 x 4½ x ½ in [15.0 x 11.3 x 1.3 cm]): Altered book including found poetry and original painted and drawn artwork, paper weaving and stitching, and collages of mixed media including ephemera, tea bags, mica, copper wire, coffee filters, and moss.

0106, 0107 **Embalm** (7¼ x 5½ x ¾ in [18.1 x 13.8 x 1.9 cm]): Two cedar tablets bound with waxed thread, with archival inkjet prints of an original poem and charcoal drawing embedded in encaustic wax.

0108, 0109 **Paper** (3¼ x 2¾ x 1¼ in [8.1 x 6.9 x 3.1 cm]): Inkjet prints of a poem by Joana Varawa on hanji (Korean handmade paper), sewn onto pages of spun and knitted lokta (Nepalese handmade paper), bound in naturally-dyed hanji.

0110, 0111 **In Case of Panic** (4½ x 7 x ¼ in [11.3 x 17.5 x 0.6 cm]): Original photographs shot while driving over Chesapeake Bay Bridge, printed with archival digital pigments and typewritten original text on heavyweight silkscreen paper, bound with post and screw.

0112, 0113, 0114 **Fusion Frottage [One]** (8 x 9 x ¾ in [20.0 x 22.5 x 1.9 cm]): Creative application of garbage by using recyclables as illustrations. Letterpress of type and found objects (mounted type-high on press).

0115, 0116 **White Insistence** (9 x 6¼ x 1 in [22.5 x 15.6 x 2.5 cm]): Text by Michael Burkard, letterpress-printed with subsequent page tearing by the artist, printed and bound by Mason Miller in canvas over archival board, with blind-embossed cover. The fretted edges of the pages add resonance to the fretful and obsessive subject of the story.

0117, 0118, 0119 **Don't Blame Pandora (for the Atomic Bomb and Atomic Age)** (11 x 8½ x ½ in [27.5 x 21.3 x 1.3 cm]): Original text and illustrations created with a Japanese paper drill.

0120 **Tea Bag Books** (5 x 5¼ x 1 in [12.5 x 13.1 x 2.5 cm]): Shellacked tea bags, machine sewn with black thread, with coptic bound interior of handmade paper.

0121, 0122, 0123 **There Goes the Neighborhood** (10½ x 8¾ x 1¼ in [26.3 x 21.9 x 3.1 cm]): Scanned and manipulated nineteenth century engravings and original text, inkjet-printed on paper and transparencies, illustrating human impact upon environment.

0124, 0125 **Psychic Research** (18 x 15 x ¾ in [45.0 x 37.5 x 1.9 cm]): Original acrylic paintings and solvent transfers with found objects on canvas, with original paper and canvas collaged text. French door binding.

0126, 0127 **Neon** (7 x 10 x 1½ in [17.5 x 25.0 x 3.8 cm]): Original silver gelatin prints and painted wire sculptures bound with dyed Tyvek; cover of galvanized steel sheet over board with painted wire title. Opens 360°.

0128, 0129 **My Brain Uses Numbers for….** (4 x 11 x ½ in [10.0 x 27.5 x 1.3 cm]): Laser and letterpress printing with original collages on laid kraft paper and corrugated cardboard.

0130 **Closed** (4 x 2 x ½ in [10.0 x 5.0 x 1.3 cm]): Paper slide mounts and kraft paper bound with turkey rings (split plastic rings used by turkey farmers), containing collages of various closures (key, wax seal, safety pin, etc.).

0131, 0132 **Meaning** (3 x 2¾ x ½ in [7.5 6.9 x 1.3 cm]): Miniature codex featuring text by the artist and by Jorge Luis Borges, Emily Dickinson, and Walt Whitman, with found illustrations from Dissector in Abstract combined with collage, inkjet prints, watercolors, and ink pen. Magnetic bead closure.

0133, 0134 **The Value of Secrets** (6 x 8 x 2 in [15.0 x 20.0 x 5.0 cm]): Bundled stitch book, loose handmade felt pages and a glass object contained in a handmade two-piece box. Original handwritten and needlefelted text and acrylic ink painted papers. Other materials include Mylar and shredded money.

0135, 0136 **The Child with a Bent Spine** (7¼ x 5¼ x ⅓ in [18.1 x 13.1 x 0.8 cm]): Original text and illustrations silk screened and offset printed, silk bookcloth cover.

0137, 0138 **Forest** (8¼ x 10 in [20.6 x 25.0 cm]): Original pinhole photography and poems by Mary Agnes Williams; artist's original linocut prints and woodcut prints, with 3D hardbound cover of cut, painted, and laminated paper.

0139, 0140 **River** (2¾ x 3⅛ x ⅛ in [6.9 x 7.8 x 0.3 cm]): Hand-dyed cloth cover, marbled and Japanese paper interior, computer-printed original text.

0141, 0142, 0143 **Manifest, O** (18½ x 13½ x 4 in [46.3 x 33.8 x 10.0 cm]): A visual interpretation of experiencing hearing loss. Cover of cast kozo, Pergamena vellum, sanded goatskin, bamboo, and dyes. Interior of handmade abaca paper with hand-formed "text-holes," hand-stained and sized, featuring original Prismacolor pencil illustrations.

0144, 0145 **Spirit Book #35: Earthy Radiance** (14 x 18½ x 7½ in [35.0 x 46.3 x 18.8 cm]): Handmade paper from Bhutan, Lokta paper from Nepal, Mashamba paper from Africa, seed beads and thread, and grapvine tendrils on a base of binders board and paper, held in a cradle of grape vines.

0146, 0147 **Third Party, Fire and Theft** (5⅛ x 8 x ½ in [12.8 x 20.0 x 1.3 cm]): Original rubber-stamped text on kitchen cloths and abaca paper with hand-applied inks and wax.

0148, 0149 **Harbinger** (6 x 4 x 1½ in [15.0 x 10.0 x 3.8 cm]): Original text and illustrations created with mixed media incuding watercolor, gold and silver crayons, and wax on basswood with a silk-covered slip case.

0150, 0151 **At the Beach** (8⁵⁄₁₆ x 8¼ x 4⅛ in [20.8 x 21.1 x 10.5 cm]): Multiple volumes of digitally printed original photographs and poetry bound back-to-back.

0152, 0153, 0154 **Mexico Stories** (8½ x 10½ x ¾ in [21.3 x 26.3 x 1.9 cm]): Original calligraphy and deconstructed paper painting, with charms and beads on wooden spine.

0155, 0156 **The Sacred Abecedarium** (11½ x 8¾ x ¾ in [28.8 x 21.9 x 1.9 cm]): Original reduction block prints by the artist and Steven Ferlauto on Brian Borchardt's handmade paper. Letterpress printed text by Steven Ferlauto, with collage and watercolors.

0157, 0158 **This Time** (3 x 2½ x ¾ in [7.5 x 6.3 x 1.9 cm]): Dropspine box with stiff-leaf hardcover binding, original text and illustrations printed with color intaglio.

0159, 0160 **The Pygmy Owl Is Disappearing** (5 x 9 x 1 in [12.5 x 22.5 x 2.5 cm]): Piano-hinge binding of artist's handmade paper (abaca, canna and pigment), original ink drawings, and original stamped text.

0161, 0162 **Fly Away Home** (5 x 5½ x 2 in [12.5 x 13.8 x 5.0 cm]): Cover made from antique wooden baseboard, collage, and acrylic;

interior printed with hand-set type on a letterpress and hand-carved wood block prints.

0163 **Fish Out of Water** (4½ x 6 x ½ in [11.3 x 15.0 x 1.3 cm]): Polymer clay cover with pages of thin sheets of translucent polymer clay with transferred images.

0164, 0165 **Hecatombe 9-11** (11 x 4¼ x 2 in [27.5 x 10.6 x 5.0 cm]): A memorial book on the 9/11 attacks on the US. Two codex structures symbolize the Twin Towers of NYC, listing victims' names alphabetically. An accordion wall of photographs taken by the artist connects them. The title is laser cut creating a symbolic void. End sheets relief-printed in silver ink. Laser printed and housed in a phase box with a stenciled fallen towers image.

0166, 0167, 0168 **Euxoa Auxiliaris** (3½ x 2½ x 1⅛ in [8.8 x 6.3 x 2.8 cm]): Mongolian-style rigid book with pages of poplar covered with Cave paper. Each page holds a recessed plastic box with a Miller moth inside. Original laser-printed text, and mixed media including color reproductions and mica.

0169, 0170 **Relative Remains** (2½ x 2½ x 1¼ in [6.3 x 6.3 x 3.1 cm]): Exposed spine hand-sewn hardcover in slipcase, original text and illustrations printed with archival inkjet and intaglio.

0171, 0172 **Journey In White** (5½ x 4½ x ¼ in [13.8 x 11.3 x 0.6 cm]): Original text and dresses scanned and inkjet printed on handmade paper and stitched to fabric backing; cover of handmade gampi over fabric.

0173, 0174, 0175 **Abcé (Mexico City Book 2)** (5¼ x 7¼ x ½ in [13.1 x 18.1 x 1.3 cm]): Original photographs Indigo digital printing, handmade covers, and quarter cloth with Amaté paper.

0176, 0177 **Azusa: a sequel** (9¾ x 6½ x ¾ in [24.4 x 16.3 x 1.9 cm]): Poetry by Paul Vangelisti letterpress printed using assorted wood type and photopolymer plates. Cover of Harmatan goat leather with hand-sewn silk endbands.

0178 **Mutually Assured Destruction** (7¼ x 5½ x ½ in [18.1 x 13.8 x 1.3 cm]): Photocopy transfers of digitally-manipulated found images, accordion spine structure.

0179, 0180 **Collateral Damage [Uncorrected]** (7⅛ x 16¾ x ½ in [17.8 x 41.9 x 1.3 cm]): Lint from USA flags on lint roller sheets with correction fluid used to transcribe letters from Major Sullivan Ballou (died at the Battle of Bull Run, July 21, 1861; letter dated July 14, 1861) and PFC Jesse Givens (died at Al Habbaniyah, Iraq, May 1, 2003; letter dated April 22, 2003).

0181, 0182 **Books & Changes** (22½ x 9 x 3½ in [56.3 x 22.5 x 8.8 cm]): Canson paper sandwiched between Kodalith negatives of phototypeset dream narrative text and James Petrillo's Cibachrome prints. Folios with wire edges are inserted into metal strips screwed to a wood base.

0183, 0184 **The Imperial Inn** (5½ x 3½ x 1 in [13.8 x 8.8 x 2.5 cm]): Sterling silver cover, texturized with a needle file, with soldered hinges. Interior pages of sterling silver rolled through a mill, then typed on a ribbonless typewriter.

0185, 0186 **The Khmer Legacy** (21 x 12 x 3¼ in [52.5 x 30.0 x 8.1 cm]): Pop-up book made from inkjet prints, mulberry paper, collage, and hand-coloring.

0187, 0188 **It Is Not** (11 x 11 x ½ in [27.5 x 27.5 x 1.3 cm]): Original calligraphy of a poem by Quincy Troupe, with illumination with gold leaf, collage, and illustration with sumi and resist on Rives lightweight text pages. Cover of handmade Cave paper.

0189, 0190 **Curious Beaks** (⅝ x 1 x ⅜ in [1.6 x 2.5 x 0.9 cm]): Miniature book bound with an antiqued cover featuring digital typography and housed in a custom brass and copper box; interior features vintage images from John Player & Sons that have been digitally edited and laser printed.

0191, 0192 **ABC Trees** (1½ x 1⅛ x ⅕ in [3.8 x 2.8 x 0.5 cm]): Miniature book featuring original photography of tree branches forming the letters of the alphabet; laser printed interior, bound with a cover of suminagashi marbled paper over boards, and housed in a brass flip-frame case.

0193, 0194 **At Home Again: a miniature book of Victorian children's poetry** (1¾ x 1½ x ⅛ in [4.4 x 3.8 x 0.3 cm]): Miniature book in a clamshell box. Text by Eliza Keary with illustrations by J.G. Sowerby. Leather cover with inlayed picture, marbled end papers, printed on Novatech paper on a digital press.

0195, 0196 **Spells and Potions** (⅚ x ⅔ x ⅙ in [2.1 x 1.7 x 0.4 cm]): A miniature book of home remedies illustrated with herbs. Original text printed on Novatech paper on a digital press. Various illustrators. Leather cover with blind tooling, marbled end papers.

0197, 0198 **Mahô Nikki (Magic Diary)** (2⅝ x 2 x 4/9 in [6.6 x 5.0 x 1.1 cm]): Miniature book with letterpress printed original text and handmade Japanese paper.

0199 **A Time for Small Things** (1⅘ x 1⅖ x ½ in [4.5 x 3.5 x 1.3 cm]): Miniature book with text by Miguel de Cervantes Saavedra, on a chain. Pearls, crystals, glass, and antique metal beads on silk. Digitally printed interior pages.

0200, 0201, 0202 **32 Studies** (3⅛ x 2 ¾ in [7.8 x 6.9 cm]): Calf spine stamped in gold; acrylic and lacquer boards, three edges gilt. Interior original paintings in acrylic, watercolor, inks, and gold tooling on handmade paper.

0203 **A Book for Anne Bradstreet** (6¾ x 7½ x ¾ in [16.9 x 18.8 x 1.9 cm]): Hand-set 4-color letterpress printed text by Ann Bradstreet with original commentary and hand-embroidery by the artist using seventeenth century style stitching.

0204, 0205, 0206 **Wallet Book** (3¼ x 4¼ x ½ in [8.1 x 10.6 x 1.3 cm]): Original typewritten text, gelatin silver photographs, and letterpress printed original art pamphlet book in a wallet.

0207, 0208 **Silence Is an Orchard** (15 x 11 x 4/9 in [37.5 x 27.5 x 1.1 cm]): Original pigment print photographs of one field in Maine on Japanese kozo paper with a poem by Kirsten Rian. Cover with original etching by Sarah Horowitz on Bhutan Mitsumata paper.

0209 **Lost with a Map** (9½ x 4 in [23.8 x 10.0 cm]): Letterpress book containing six pressure prints and an original essay by the artist, referencing the journey and finding one's way. It is about language and communication, and how words can fail us in understanding.

0210, 0211 **Balancing the Fear and the Pleasure of Food** (11½ x 17½ x 1 in [28.8 x 43.8 x 2.5 cm]): Cover of repurposed textiles, hand-stitched embroidery, and screen printing. Interior of text used with permission from *Nourishing Traditions Cookbook* by Sally Fallon along with artist's original handwritten text. Screen printing in collaboration with Jenny Ankeny, Print Gocco in collaboration with Shu-Ju Wang.

0212 **Alabama Kitchen: Recipes for the Southerner and Southerner-at-heart** (8 x 6¾ x 1 in [20.0 x 16.9 x 2.5 cm]): Artist-collected recipes from three farms with illustrations by Lucy Player letterpress printed with photopolymer plates. Cover and slipcase covered with Artist's handmade abaca/cotton paper dyed with handmade walnut dye. Conceptualized as a utilitarian fine press book.

0213, 0214 **Fat Chance** (6½ x 6 x 3¾ in [16.3 x 15.0 x 9.4 cm]): Reclaimed diet pamphlets sewn all-along on leather belts, with painted edges and double French endbands. Nigerian goat cover with measuring tape and Fabriano Roma.

0215, 0216 **Fortune Cookie Rose** (3 x 5½ x 1½ in [7.5 x 13.8 x 3.8 cm]): Stitched collages in a cover of stitched fabric layers backed with decorative paper and a button closure.

0217, 0218 **Frustration** (9½ x 12 x 11 in [23.8 x 30.0 x 27.5 cm]): Cooked, beaten, and hand-sculpted handmade Kozo paper cover, with an interior of original text on handmade Kozo sheets typed with vintage typewriter.

0219, 0220, 0221 **Book of Qamar** (9⅝ x 9¼ x 1¼ in [24.1 x 23.1 x 3.1 cm]): Sewn round book with original drawn and painted illustrations in acrylic ink on goatskin pages, in a goatskin wrapper.

0222, 0223 **Paste Paper Stripes** (2⅝ x 2⅜ x ½ in [6.6 x 5.9 x 1.3 cm]): Cover of artist's painted paste papers with exposed sewing cutout. Interior pages of paste paper strips and digital printing on folded pages sewn on linen tapes.

0224 **Beyond Compare** (3 x 3 x 15 in [7.5 x 7.5 x 37.5 cm]): Sewn Slinky-style book including handwriting, drawing, and painting throughout interior, and a wall-sized US Geological Survey map of Mammoth Cave National Park on pages' exterior. Cover includes Indian handmade cotton paper, and page interiors are black Tyvek. Text and images concern Mammoth Cave.

0225, 0226 **Our Own Version of Journey to the Center of the Earth** (5¼ x 5¼ x 5¼ in [13.1 x 13.1 x 13.1 cm]): Artist's young daughter's version of Jules Verne's *Journey to the Center of the Earth*, inkjet printed on watercolor paper. Edition of 20.

0227, 0228 **Midnight Haiku** (3 x 2⅝ x ¾ in [7.5 x 6.6 x 1.9 cm]): Hemp paper, painted with acrylic paint, with painted silk appliqué, seed beads, and embroidery. Sewn over tape binding.

0229, 0230 **Walks with Rosie** (15 x 11 x ½ in [37.5 x 27.5 x 1.3 cm]): Printed with original linoleum cuts, hand-set letterpress printing, and pochoir on Sekishu tissue, based on artist's walks with his dog. Bound in cloth and paper.

0231 **A Strawberry in the Snow** (6½ x 4¾ x 1 in [16.3 x 11.9 x 2.5 cm]): Poems and illustrations about the nature of familial relationships. Letterpress printed from photopolymer plates and linoleum cut blocks on Hahnemühle Biblio and Kitakata. Text by Leah Eisenbeis. French-sewn binding in a full-cloth, built-in groove, flat-back case, enclosed in a handmade clamshell box.

0232, 0233, 0234 **St. Raphael** (10½ x 7⅓ x ⅓ in [26.3 x 18.3 x 0.8 cm]): Original calligraphy of selected text from a Federico Garcia Lorca poem translated by Will Kirkland, with illumination, collage, and painting on Rives BFK text pages. Cover made from B-9 handmade paper from the University of Iowa Paper Facility.

0235 **Failures/Success** (4 x 6 x ⅛ in [10.0 x 15.0 x 0.3 cm]): Original hand-drawn text and imagery, offset printed on French Paper Company's Pop-Tone paper; dos-à-dos structure.

0236, 0237, 0238 **Connect the Outer Ring** (15 x 11 x ½ in [37.5 x 27.5 x 1.3 cm]): Original paintings and drawings in ink, watercolor, graphite, acrylics, and gold on leather and paper. Drum leaf binding.

0239, 0240, 0241 **Abandon** (7 x 5 x 1 in [17.5 x 12.5 x 2.5 cm]): Adhered folios of digital pigment prints of original photographs and text by an anonymous author; painted wood and ribbon cover.

0242 **Dream** (5⅝ x 5½ x ⅞ in [14.3 x 14 x 2.2 cm]): Modified stiff-leaf binding with original woodblock prints, text, and collage in a clam shell box.

0243, 0244 **The Return** (11 x 6 x 2 in [27.5 x 15.0 x 5.0 cm]): Poetry by Felip Costaglioli. Painted pages are done in oil on Rives BFK paper. Typography is hand-lettered with graphite. Drum-leaf binding in a clamshell case with linen spine.

0245, 0246 **Urban Landscapes** (4 x 3 x ½ in [10.0 x 7.5 x 1.3 cm]): Drum leaf-bound linoleum block prints, low-relief pressure prints, and letterpress from photopolymer plates on Rives BFK.

0247, 0248, 0249 **The Articifer Arisen, the Articifer Fallen** (7 x 7 x 1½ in [17.5 x 17.5 x 3.8 cm]): Drum leaf bound dos-à-dos structure with original text and illustrations letterpress printed in three colors on handmade cotton/flax. Cover of book cloth, beeswax, faux-suede, and hemp thread.

0250, 0251 **Cliqued** (6 x 9 x ½ in [15.0 x 22.5 x 1.3 cm]): Digitally manipulated original photographs and original text printed with archival pigments on matte cover paper; drum leaf binding. Depicting memories of conformity and belonging.

0252, 0253, 0254 **The Well** (15 x 9½ x 1 in [37.5 x 23.8 x 2.5 cm]): Original paintings and drawings in acrylics, ink, and watercolor on paper. Iron, gold, and acrylic materials on Egyptian cotton and paper on a drum leaf binding.

0255, 0256, 0257 **If You Dive Deep Enough You Can See the Stars** (19 x 7 in [47.5 x 17.5 cm]): Original letterpress printed text and monoprints. Cover of silk and letterpress printing; Page as Hinge binding.

0258, 0259 **A Biography of a Modern Woman** (8 x 6 x ½ in [20.0 x 15.0 x 1.3 cm]): Original woodcuts and collage with original digitally printed text and pop-up elements. Cover of handmade denim paper over boards with digital printing. Drum leaf binding.

0260, 0261, 0262 **Shelter** (11 x 8½ x ⅝ in [27.5 x 21.3 x 1.6 cm]): An accordion-fold structure inside a codex book, original text and photography printed with Indigo-imaged paper, hand-sewn binding with hand-cut windows.

0263, 0264 **Rorschach's Animals** (2¾ x 5 in [6.9 x 12.5 cm]): Original collage and inkblots, photocopied and bound with linen tape with a Barnum's Animal Crackers box cover.

0265, 0266 **Beautiful Tattoos** (4¼ x 10 x ¾ in [10.6 x 25.0 x 1.9 cm]): Single signature of handmade wool wet-felted pages, original text, and images created by needlefelting.

0267, 0268 **An Illuminated Book of Cats** (9 x 6¾ x 1⅞ in [22.5 x 16.9 x 4.7 cm]): Artist's original illustrations with text by Rod Morgan, printed digitally on watercolor paper with hand-applied gold leaf and hand-deckled edges. Cover of leather over relief-sculpted boards. Coptic bound.

0269, 0270 **My Ice Cream Book** (4 x 5 x ¾ in [10.0 x 12.5 x 1.9 cm]): Original calligraphy, drawings, and watercolor on Canson Mi-Teintes, bound in a cover of St. Armand handmade paper with a wooden ice cream stick stitched in the binding.

0271, 0272, 0273 **1001010, 01101111, 01111001 (Joy)** (10¾ x 6⅝ x 1¾ in [26.9 x 16.6 x 4.4 cm]): Hand-lettering and brush marks in sumi and walnut inks, gold acrylic paint, MacGreggor Vinzanni paper, and painted woven Tyvek. Includes music by Beethoven, writings by Schiller, and binary code.

0274 **Leaves of Irony** (4 x 2½ x ¼ in [10.0 x 6.3 x 0.6 cm]): Weathered, galvanized iron with a nonadhesive visible binding using found materials.

0275, 0276 **Crumpling a Thin Sheet** (15 x 14½ x 1¼ in [37.5 x 36.3 x 3.1 cm]): Text from of a complete scientific article written by Matan, Williams, Witten, and Nagel, illustrated with original photographs of paper that was crumpled in precisely measured amounts. Digital scans and inkjet printing on Velin Arches Blanc; sewn binding.

0277 **Duotone #2** (13 x 9¼ x 6 in [32.5 x 23.1 x 15.0 cm]): Form accentuated in black and white through two-needle Coptic binding of Canson paper, Chromo bookcloth, Davey bookboard, decorative paper, and linen threads.

0278, 0279 **Souvenir from Casteldefels** (13 x 18 x ½ in [32.5 x 45.0 x 1.3 cm]): Found objects, black India ink, and linen thread on a single signature of Polish linen.

0280 **Elevated Threat** (5 x 3½ x 1 in [12.5 x 8.8 x 2.5 cm]): Collaged digital transfers on painted boards with found photoengraving.

0281 **Concatenation** (12 x 8 x 3 in [30.0 x 20.0 x 7.5 cm]): Relief printed ceramic covers with hand-impressed wood and metal types in side-stitched sculptural bookform incorporating a found encyclopedia.

0282, 0283 **Burning Holes III** (2½ x 3⅜ x ½ in [6.3 x 8.4 x 1.3 cm]): Double-sided layered and carved paste paper with burnt holes providing extra views. Original binding on threads.

0284, 0285 **Home Ground** (8½ x 16 x 3 in [21.3 x 40.0 x 7.5 cm]): Original inkjet printed photos on photo paper and handmade yucca paper, leaf printing on yucca paper, hand-stitching, and various handmade photo alterations, with a bark frame.

0286 **Tree Book** (5 x 4½ x 3 in [12.5 x 11.3 x 7.5 cm]): Woodburned alphabetical list of trees on pieces of wood with a bark and leather binding.

0287, 0288 **Lost in the Hurricanes** (2¾ x 1¼ x ½ in [6.9 x 3.1 x 1.3 cm]): Codex containing original encaustic monoprints housed in an encaustic frame, in remembrance of houses lost in hurricanes.

0289, 0290 **Hypnotism Hand Book** (6¼ x 3¼ x 1½ in [15.6 x 8.1 x 3.8 cm]): Stick-bound, collaged, and machine-stitched split pages with Cave paper covers

0291, 0292 **I Saw the Number 5 in Gold** (5½ x 3½ x 4½ in [13.8 x 8.8 x 11.3 cm]): Board book including collage, drawing, painting, sanding, stenciling, and frotage on various papers with found objects.

0293 **Hokusai No Yūrei (Hokusai's Ghost)** (5½ x 11 x 45 in [13.8 x 27.5 x 112.5 cm]): One-needle Coptic binding of Canson paper, bookcloth, Davey bookboard, cotton cords, and linen threads, capturing the essence of the story.

0294, 0295, 0296 **Girl of Glass** (4 x 3 x ⅜ in [10.0 x 7.5 x 0.9 cm]): Original text digitally printed on vellum with an etched glass cover. Conceptually illustrates love, shame, and acceptance.

0297, 0298 **The Invisible Man** (8¾ x 5¾ x 2 in [21.9 x 14.4 x 5.0 cm]): Text of H.G. Wells' *The Invisible Man* laser-printed on transparencies, with inserted color transparencies of human biological images. Open spine binding sewn with kite string; etched acrylic presentation box.

0299 **Incantamenta** (4½ x 3½ x ¾ in [11.3 x 8.8 x 1.9 cm]): Ancient spells in Latin and Greek on sanded salt dough tablet pages; original illustration on the cover.

0300, 0301, 0302 **Prophet** (6 x 4¾ x 1 in [15.0 x 11.9 x 2.5 cm]): Bookboard (commercial children's book, sanded down to remove images), with inked collage parts and graphite juxtaposing deity-like figures and text relationships.

0303, 0304 **Pattern Trilogy I II III** (7⅞ x 3 x ¼ in [19.7 x 7.5 x 0.6 cm]): Set of three stab-bound books with covers of recycled Japanese paper and incuding stamples, stencils, and original drawings.

0305, 0306 **Wabi Sabi** (19¾ x 19 x 1 in [49.4 x 47.5 x 2.5 cm]): Original computer-printed text and original illlustrations of batik painting, colored pencil, graphite, and rusting on the artist's handmade paper with seed pods, nails, twine, and bamboo to examine the traditional Japanese aesthetic of Wabi Sabi.

0307, 0308 **Bilingual ABC Bilingüe** (5½ x 8½ x ½ in [13.8 x 21.3 x 1.3 cm]): Hand-stitched original linocut prints with a cardboard cover.

0309, 0310 **Scarecrows** (7 x 5¼ x ½ in [17.5 x 13.1 x 1.3 cm]): Text by Daniel Defoe (from *Robinson Crusoe*) with digital illustrations inkjet printed on Somerset Velvet and Kraft papers, stab-bound with wooden stick and embroidery thread.

0311 **Tsunami** (9 x 1½ x 1½ in [22.5 x 3.8 x 3.8 cm]): Original Sumi ink wash on Japanese paper with a leather cover.

0312, 0313 **Pulp, A Love Story: My Serbian Affair with Papermaking** (7½ x 9¾ x ¼ in [18.8 x 24.4 x 0.6 cm]): Original comic illustrations and text by Vlada Veljasević and primer by Potter about the hand-papermaking process in an offset-printed tête-bêche structure.

0314, 0315 **A Winter's Tale** (3¼ x 5⅛ x 1¼ in [8.1 x 12.8 x 3.1 cm]): Raised cord binding, using hemp cord, St. Armand paper, and hand-embossed mulberry papers. Title typewritten on an antique typewriter.

0316, 0317, 0318 **ABKey** (4 x 4 x 1½ in [10.0 x 10.0 x 3.8 cm]): Alphabet board book of original colored pencil drawings, scanned and printed with hand-crayoned details on Hammermill paper and board, detailing the complex life of the girl who owns it as she transitions from girlhood to womanhood.

0319, 0320 **El Alfabeto Animado (The Lively Alphabet / Uywakunawan Qelqasqa)** (19¾ x 25½ x 3 in [49.4 x 63.8 x 7.5 cm]): Japanese stab binding of bayeta (woolen cloth from Cusco, Peru) with text by Mondica Brown and illustrations by Felicia Rice, letterpress printed from wooden type and photoengravings of charcoal drawings. Jenny Callañaupa Huarhua, translator. Katie Jennings, muse.

0321, 0322, 0323 **Neverwhere** (6¾ x 4¼ x 2 in [17.0 x 10.6 x 5.0 cm]): Altered steampunk book (authored by Neil Gaiman), and design binding. Binding of copper, brass, copper leaf, mica, brass nails, and rivets. Interior pages treated with inks and image transfers.

0324, 0325 **Scripta Naturae** (17 x 13 x ¾ in [42.5 x 32.5 x 1.9 cm]): Design binding for Ladislav Hanka's *Scripta Naturae*. Original etchings, chagrin leather spine, book edges, and edges of cut outs. Decorative papers by the late Claude Del Pierre, magnets, and gold.

0326 **Poselstvi Dreva** (14 x 10 x 2½ in [35.0 x 25.0 x 6.3 cm]): Text by Vaclav Splichal illustrated by a group of Czech artists, bound in 8 different wood panels, wood sculpture, and leather.

0327 **The Art of the Book** (11½ x 8¼ x 1½ in [28.8 x 20.6 x 3.8 cm]): A modern adaptation of traditional panel binding sewn with Japanese, Czech, and Italian beads into floss-embroidered velveteen. *The Art of the Book: A Review of Some Recent European and American Work in Typography, Page Decoration and Binding,* 1914, references the historical embroidered book.

0328 **Gardener's Journal** (5½ x 4¼ x 2⅓ in [13.8 x 10.6 x 5.5 cm]): Tooled leather-covered boards and cotton/linen text paper bound on cords.

0329, 0330 **The Children of Lir** (3½ x 7 x 3 in [8.8 x 17.5 x 7.5 cm]): Carved wood cover with leather spine and supported stitching on cords, containing an Irish legend and original photographs of swans.

0331, 0332 **Over the Edge: Death in Grand Canyon** (9¼ x 6½ x 1¾ in [23.1 x 16.3 x 4.4 cm]): Design binding for book by Thomas M. Myers and Michael P. Ghiglieri. Full leather goatskin binding, gilt edge, onlays, and carbon tooling.

0333 **A History of the Moon** (8 x 6⅛ x ⅝ in [20.0 x 15.3 x 1.6 cm]): Design binding for *A History of the Moon* by Alvey Jones, with illustrations by the author. Long grain chagrin goat skin leather with inlays of eggshell on the front, and of box calf leather on the back. Palladium tooling on the front.

0334 **Embraceable Object** (9 x 22 x 3 in [22.5 x 55.0 x 7.5 cm]): Modified oriental binding of oversized book with leather cover, clasp from antique door knocker and inset objects.

0335 **Dante's Inferno** (16 x 12 x 1 in [40.0 x 30.0 x 2.5 cm]): Binding for *Dante's Inferno* by Tom Philips. Blind tooled calf dyed by the artist. Bronze bosses and centerpieces cast from Ashanti gold weights in Philips' collection; brass clasps engraved with the Florentine lily and hands drawn by Tom Philips.

0336, 0337 **Billy Budd Sailor** (10 x 6½ x ¾ in [25.0 x 16.3 x 1.9 cm]): English-style leather binding with low-relief sculpture set into the front cover, scarf-joined dyed vegetable-tanned goatskin leather. Contains letterpress printed text by Herman Melville and engravings by Deborah Alterman.

0338 **Gardening in the South** (6 x 4 x 2 in [15.0 x 10.0 x 5.0 cm]): Pieced and appliquéd leather-covered boards sewn with silk thread, and holding commercial, coffee-dyed papers bound on cords.

0339 **Le Jardinier** (14 x 13½ x ½ in [35.0 x 33.8 x 1.3 cm]): Design binding for *Le Jardinier* by Michel van Schendel with illustrations by Louis-Pierre Bougie. Goat skin leather with inlays of stingray fish skin, onlays of goat skin leather, and gold tooling.

0340, 0341 **Through the Looking Glass** (12 x 11 x 2½ in [30.0 x 27.5 x 6.3 cm]): Design binding for Lewis Carroll's *Through the Looking Glass* of various leathers (French Cape Morocco, Chagrin, Oasis, frog, reptile skins, and goat suede), with abalone, magnets, gold, and palladium.

0342, 0343 **Crows on Bare Branches** (8¼ x 5¼ x ⅝ in [20.6 x 13.1 x 1.6 cm]): Hand-set letterpress type of original text by Tom Sexton and original woodcuts by the artist on Johannot mouldmade paper with Twinrocker handmade paper covers. Encased in an Asahi bookcloth covered chemise.

0344, 0345 **Ripped** (9 x 10 x 1 in [22.5 x 25.0 x 2.5 cm]): Original text composed by wordle.net word cloud software digitally printed on handmade recycled paper with added pulp painting.

0346, 0347 **The Thread that Binds** (9¼ x 5 x 3¾ in [23.1 x 12.5 x 9.4 cm]): Asahi silk with silk threads in the valleys of the cover. Interior is a commercially-printed book by Pamela Train Leutz.

0348, 0349 **In the Cupboard** (4⅓ x 7¾ x 1¼ in [10.8 x 19.4 x 3.1 cm]): Handmade felt made from two years of clothes dryer lint with original linoprints and rubber stamps.

0350, 0351 **Letter from a Desert** (8¼ x 8¼ x ½ in [20.6 x 20.6 x 1.3 cm]): Single pages of tissue paper dipped in beeswax, stitched on one side, with found objects.

0352, 0353 **Cincuenta y uno familias: Cincuenta y uno años: A Collaboration with Cuban Families** (5¼ x 3¼ x 6¼ in [13.1 x 8.1 x 15.6 cm]): Letterpress with pencil, pen, and ink. Made in the fifty-first year of the Cuban Revolution and includes 51 libretas (family ration books) that were entrusted to the artist.

0354 **Tall Tales and Short Stories**: Collection of books made with wood, mixed mouldmade papers, acrylic paint, woodburning, and other media. Each book features the artist's original fiction based on the ups and downs of the main character, Jilly Barnes.

0355 **Mica Flags** (7 x 3 x ½ in [17.5 x 7.5 x 1.3 cm]): Mica flag book featuring naturally occurring markings.

0356, 0357, 0358 **Destination Moon** (7 x 5 x ¾ in [17.5 x 12.5 x 1.9 cm]): Flag book with photographs courtesy of NASA and text by John F. Kennedy and Roy Alfred inkjet printed on Hahnemühle and Mohawk papers.

0359 **The Postmodernist Critique** (20 x 16 x 3 in [50.0 x 40.0 x 7.5 cm]): Flag book featuring Kurt Cobain lyrics, "Oh well. Whatever. Never mind." in ink on artist's paste paper, each flag with linen thread.

0360, 0361 **Fossil Fuels** (7½ x 3 in [18.8 x 7.5 cm]): Cover of handmade denim paper, embroidered interior Rives BFK paper featuring original collograph and intaglio prints and digital printing.

0362, 0363 **Dirty Dancing** (10 x 10 x ½ in [25.0 x 25.0 x 1.3 cm]): Original watercolor artwork and calligraphy on Canson paper, leather cover with onlay.

0364 **Hit The Road!** (9 x 5¾ x 1 in [22.5 x 14.4 x 2.5 cm]): Single layer flag book of original photographs of roadside artifacts on Highway 99 in Washington printed with archival pigments on Mohawk Superfine paper, Arches Mi-Tientes paper, and Iris book cloth.

0365, 0366 **The Phoenix** (7½ x 7½ x ½ in [18.8 x 18.8 x 1.3 cm]): Exerpts from *The Exeter Book* with an English translation by Benjamin Thorpe, vignettes and calligraphy by Cathy Ledeker, relief cuts by Linda Samson-Talleur.

0367, 0368, 0369 **The Art of Language** (13 x 5½ x 6 in [32.5 x 13.8 x 15.0 cm]): Hedi Kyle panel book with Redwood block covers, text designed on computer and printed on commercial papers, with original paste paper.

0370, 0371, 0372 **Good Will & Salvation** (5 x 5 x 15 in [12.5 x 12.5 x 37.5 cm]): Woven accordion struction of original photographs documenting thrift store finds and consumer culture, printed with archival pigments on Moab Entrada and Moab Lasal digital papers.

0373 **The Beads in My Hand** (6 x 6 x 2 in [15 x 15 x 5 cm]): Inkjet printing of original images, with beads and magnets.

0374, 0375 **The Coaching Book** (5 x 3⅜ x ⅝ in [12.5 x 8.4 x 1.6 cm]): Original monoprints on kozo paper with covers of silk on board.

0376 **Pearls Before Swine** (4½ x 7 x 2 in [11.3 x 17.5 x 5.0 cm]): Coil-bound accordion-fold dos-à-dos of deconstructed and riveted tin litho cans with copper hinges, milagros, and other found objects.

0377 **Pyramid Book** (5 x 5 x ½ in [12.5 x 12.5 x 1.3 cm]): Calf skin case with brass sewing key, mixed media pages with knotted rod binding.

0378 **Tetsubin (a brief history of Japanese cast iron kettles)** (4¾ x 4¾ x ½ in [11.9 x 11.9 x 1.3 cm]): Fourteen original hand-carved block prints on the artist's handmade konnyaku-treated hickory paper with a watermarked cover pattern.

0379 **You Me Us We** (7 x 2 x 1 in [17.5 x 5.0 x 2.5 cm]): Concertina/snake book with digital prints of wooden type impressions on handmade New Zealand flax and zizania papers.

0380 **Autumn Pales** (7½ x 7½ x 3⅝ in [18.8 x 18.8 x 9.1 cm]): Original text (English and shorthand) with fabric, paper, and felt, cut and sewn into a book.

0381, 0382 **Nolli** (5 x 5½ x ½ in [12.5 x 13.8 x 1.3 cm]): Original text and illustration by Alice Austin and Jon Snyder, offset lithography on cover weight paper.

0383, 0384 **Bill-Ding a Strong Foundation** (5½ x 2¼ x 1¾ in [13.8 x 5.6 x 4.4 cm]): Vintage wood Bill Ding building block covers (Stuhr Products, licensed owner of Bill Ding Balancing Clown Toys). Amate, kozo, specialty and found papers, accented with pen, ink, oil pastels, rubber stamps, and other media.

0385, 0386 **Dystopia** (9 x 4 x ½ in [22.5 x 10.0 x 1.3 cm]): A three-dimensional city emerges, unfolds, and metamorphoses. Hand-assembled linocut prints with foldable inserts.

0387, 0388 **Basso Loco** (6 x 6½ x ¾ in [15.0 x 16.3 x 1.9 cm]): Casebound in leather with a paper slipcase, paste paper, and artist's paper collages.

0389, 0390, 0391 **Garden of Eden** (11 x 5½ in [27.5 x 13.8 cm]): Black and white pigment-printed images on orange paper with copper leaf apple. Illustrations by Albrecht Durer and Simone Martini accompany the Robert Frost poem "Eden." Book is housed in a carved wooden box with an acrylic-encased specimen of poison ivy.

0392 **Artists' Book** (7½ x 9½ in [18.8 x 23.8 cm]): Original etchings tipped into an accordion structure, letterpress printed quotations by Rainer Maria Rilke, William Blake, and Epictetus. Portfolio cover of antique marbled paper and kangaroo skin.

0393, 0394, 0395 **The Mystery of the Royal Robe** (11 x 10 x 5 in [27.5 x 25.0 x 12.5 cm]): Stitched accordion-fold book with cover made from goat skin, bones, leather, and amate and specialty papers. Wood burned text on amate paper interior, with gourd, cochineal dye, silk sari, pre-columbian beads and artifacts, and other media.

0396, 0397, 0398 **Made in Hong Kong** (11 x 6¼ x 1 in [27.5 x 15.6 x 2.5 cm]): Carousel book of original collages from found and commercial materials collected during a trip to Hong Kong.

0399 **Typography Series No. 1** (5¼ x 5¼ x ½ in [13.1 x 13.1 x 1.3 cm]): Color laser printing of original altered photographs and letterpress printing with hand-set type on domestic etching paper.

0400, 0401 **Quilted Lives** (5¾ x 4 x 1½ in [14.4 x 10.0 x 3.8 cm]): Paper quilt pieces and machine stitching on bleached and walnut-dyed Lokta and Canson papers.

0402 **Quercus Codex** (7½ x 7 x 6 in [18.8 x 17.5 x 15.0 cm]): Gouache drawings and added text on found library cards in an oak log cover describe history the oak tree may have witnessed.

0403 **Hair Loss** (5 x 4 x ½ in [12.5 x 10.0 x 1.3 cm]): Casebound in leather with a paper slipcase. Interior accordion of Epson prints. End sheets with artist's hair encased are handmade abaca paper by Rachel Suntop.

0404, 0405 **Drifter** (6½ x 6½ in [16.3 x 16.3 cm]): Original illustrations cut from saturated paper (paper with resin). A poem by Mick Stern was written to accompany the image.

0406, 0407 **How Do I Love Thee?** (5⅞ x 5⅞ x ⅜ in [14.7 x 14.7 x 0.9 cm]): Laser-cut paper and archival inkjet prints of original text and illustrations by Sarah Bodman and J. P. Willis, with a cover of black linen.

0408, 0409 **A Sense of Place** (3½ x 5 x 1 in [8.8 x 12.5 x 2.5 cm]): Chinese star book of original medium format Holga and digital photographs, digitally printed on vellum with book board and handmade papers.

0410, 0411, 0412 **The Time Machine, from an alternate universe** (7⅞x 6½ x 3⅜ in [19.7 x 16.3 x 8.4 cm]): Piano hinge book with hammered copper spine and secret accordion binding, featuring hand-distressed prints of original watercolor illustrations.

0413, 0414, 0415 **The Bone Book, unearthed in the Sahara** (11 x 4⅜ x 3½ in [27.5 x 10.9 x 8.8 cm]): Piano hinge book with cover of amate paper, paper clay, and papyrus, with a poppy seedpod that holds closed the secret accordion binding. Interior features original ink drawings, distressed with inks and gouache.

0416 **Blossom at the End of the Body** (8 x 10 in [20 x 25 cm]): Artist-made kozo paper with natural pigments, featuring polymer plate etching of a poem by Beckian Fritz Goldberg.

0417, 0418 **Berlin Bestiary** (7 x 5 in [17.5 x 12.5 cm]): Two-sided pop-up theater of stone animals. Artist's digitally printed and manipulated photographs, hand-assembled pop-up inserts.

0419, 0420 **Watching a Bird Learning to Fly** (7¼ x 8½ x ½ in [18.1 x 21.3 x 1.3 cm]): Double-leaved album, with original text and images printed with pigmented inkjet ink on coated matte surface photographic paper.

0421, 0422 **Past Future** (8 x 8 in [20 x 20 cm]): Mixed media unique book, original text and drawings photocopied onto handmade paper.

0423, 0424 **Tides** (6 x 4 x ½ in [15.0 x 10.0 x 1.3 cm]): Vade mecum of original text with linoleum prints of original illustrations, hand-set metal type, handmade and paste papers, housed in a hand-knit linen bag.

0425, 0426, 0427 **Down the Rabbit Hole** (6½ x 6½ x 1 ¼ in [16.3 x 16.3 x 3.1 cm]): Tunnel book with text by Louis Carroll letterpress printed with metal type and linocuts.

0428 **The Wild Book** (6 x 8½ x ½ in [15.0 x 21.3 x 1.3 cm]): Letterpress printed title, hand rubber stamping, machine stitching, Nepalese Lokta paper, Somerset paper, Glassine paper, copper sheeting, and bookcloth. Panels are cut out by hand.

0429, 0430 **Windows II** (4¼ x 4¾ x 2½ in [10.6 x 11.9 x 6.3 cm]): Early twentieth century positive photographic glass plates hinged together with folded pages of digitally printed vellum.

0431 **Roll of the Dice** (6 x 5½ x 3 in [15.0 x 13.8 x 7.5 cm]): Tunnel book with Japanese silk bookcloth cover, original intaglio and monotype prints, and digital prints.

0432, 0433 **War Dreams** (4 x 5¾ x 2½ in [10.0 x 14.4 x 6.3 cm]): Diorama of found newspaper images, artist's personal photographs, and vintage postcard, inkjet printed and collaged with glue and wire, with original text in charcoal pencil.

0434, 0435 **Road Trips 1969/2007** (9 x 6½ x 1¼ in [22.5 x 16.3 x 3.1 cm]): Tunnel book with original serigraphy, combining family stories about undergraduate road trips. Cover composed of a road map with serigraphy, book cloth, and hinged trunk flap.

0436, 0437 **In Honor of My Grandmother's Simple Life, 2** (7½ x 5½ x 8½ in [18.8 x 13.8 x 21.3 cm]): Tunnel book with pull-out pages of digital prints of original text and illustrations on Epson Enhanced Matte paper.

0438 **ESL** (10 x 10 x 2 in [25 x 25 x 5 cm]): Tunnel book binding structure; hand-marbled Arches paper with punched alphabet, hot stamped title on Cowhide leather.

0439 **Falling Leaves** (5½ x 7½ x ¼ in [13.8 x 18.8 x 0.6 cm]): Tunnel book with four layers of digital images printed on acetate, and fall poem. Gate structure cover with magnetic closure.

0440 **Aging Gracefully** (5 x 6½ x 1½ in [12.5 x 16.3 x 3.8 cm]): Casebound in cloth with a cloth-bound hard slipcase, and an interior created with laser-cut Epson prints.

0441, 0442 **Raw South** (16 x 7 x 3 in [40.0 x 17.5 x 7.5 cm]): Pages from an old US history textbook handstitched to cotton, with image transfers, and original gouache paintings of the cotton plant growing cycle. Accented by nineteenth century bone buttons, muslin, and lace. Supported by antique spindles from an old South Carolina cotton mill.

0443 **Philadelphia Freedom** (10⅝ x 10⅝ x 1¾ in [26.6 x 26.6 x 4.4 cm]): Tunnel book of original illustrations in watercolors and silver and copper composition leaf, mixed materials including public transit passes.

0444 **Tavern in the Green** (12 x 9 x 3 in [30.0 x 22.5 x 7.5 cm]): Tunnel book with original illustrations in watercolor and gouache on Arches Paper.

0445, 0446 **In the Prime of the Season** (4 x 5½ x ⅜ in [10.0 x 13.8 x 0.9 cm]): Accordion-fold book with a piano hinge spine and multiple cut-out covers of bark paper and Tyvek, containing original calligraphy of selected passages from a poem by Peggy Geeseman and water-based media illustrations.

0447, 0448 **mah!** (6¾ x 6⅔ x ⅓ in [17.0 x 16.5 x 1.0 cm]): Hand-cut paper with experimental printing and stencils.

0449, 0450 **Boustrophedon** (5½ x 5¼ x ½ in [13.8 x 13.1 x 1.3 cm]): Original design created with water-soluble crayons on Arches cover paper, cut and folded boustrophedon-style, "as the ox plows."

0451, 0452 **Proverb** (5¼ x 6¾ x 7¼ in [13.1 x 16.9 x 18.1 cm]): Zulu proverb; original oil pastel illustrations and calligraphy on a papier-mâché base.

0453 **Fences** (11½ x 5 x 2 in [28.8 x 12.5 x 5.0 cm]): Original acrylic illustrations and digital images on handmade cotton linters and plant fiber pages, mixed media including fence post pieces.

0454, 0455 **Hanging by a Thread** (3 x 2 x 2¾ in [7.5 x 5.0 x 6.9 cm]): Original hand-stamped text on hand-rusted watercolor paper, with machine stitching, beads, and cotton thread.

0456, 0457 **Horse Power** (21 x 8 x 24 in [52.5 x 20.0 x 60.0 cm]): Letterpress printed with handset wood, metal type and ornaments with printed photopolymer plates on handmade horsehair paper, accordion bound between halves of a plastic model horse.

0458 **Peace Crane** (6 x 4 x 1½ in [15.0 x 10.0 x 3.8 cm]): Original haiku in response to Great East Japan Earthquake, 3.11. 2011, inkjet printed and hot stamp pressed with hand-set type on Japanese Echizen paper; uniquely bound in origami signatures; hot stamp pressed box.

0459 **Dancers on Stage** (16 x 6 x ⅜ in [40.0 x 15.0 x 0.9 cm]): Concertina book of 100% cotton papers, monoprinting with procien dyes and lacquers, produced during a residency with a dance company.

0460 **Alchemy** (5 x 29 x 1 in [12.5 x 72.5 x 2.5 cm]): Early twentieth century contact printing frames housing a collection of original collages made with small etchings with chine colle and ephemera.

0461, 0462 **A Fishbone of Choke Cherry** (6 x 5¼ x ¼ in [15.0 x 13.1 x 0.6 cm]): A Hedi Kyle fishbone structure unfolds to reveal the artist's wordplay, which interweaves names of birds, trees, flowers, insects, and fish into an imaginary field guide.

0463 **Dinosaur Wave** (6¾ x 6 x 1¼ in [16.9 x 15.0 x 3.1 cm]): Accordion-fold bound with wire rod and hinges, pages of brass, and copper with a heat patina.

0464, 0465 **SHIFT** (9¼ x 6¼ x ½ in [23.1 x 15.6 x 1.3 cm]): Original screenprint and collage with original letterpress text on Rives BFK for interior, Lamai Li paper over bookboard for cover.

0466, 0467 **Earth Spheres** (10½ x 6½ x 1 in [26.3 x 16.3 x 2.5 cm]): Embossed goatskin leather and artist's hand-marbled paper on cover, hand-printed original woodcuts in interior along with ditigal imagery and quotes from His Holiness the 14th Dalai Lama of Tibet and various Wikipedia sources.

0468, 0469 **Hills** (2¾ x 4 ¾ x ¾ in [6.9 x 11.9 x 1.9 cm]): Manual typewriting of original text on mulberry paper. Hardcover in black bookcloth. Original engraving on zinc, intaglio printed on Rives BFK.

0470, 0471, 0472 **Be Melting Snow** (5¾ x 5½ x ½ in [14.4 x 13.8 x 1.3 cm]): Simple poetic text by Rumi and photographs of winter trees contrast with excerpts from an art history treatise in a sequence of seven handmade paper flutter books with organza and Japanese paper pages and Sycamore bark spines.

0473 **Exploring Rilke's Morgue** (6⅓ x 6⅓ x 1½ in [15.8 x 15.8 x 3.8 cm]): Original calligraphy of a Rainer Maria Rilke poem in ink and gouache on handmade paper.

0474 **The Beginning of Wisdom** (21 x 20 x 1 in [52.5 x 50.0 x 2.5 cm]): Collage of found stamps on book board with acrylic and book cloth, containing text reproduced from a letter written by Willard Bleem.

0475, 0476, 0477 **Invented Landscape** (5 x 9¾ x 1¾ in [12.5 x 24.4 x 4.4 cm]): Original text and artwork, printed using a combination of letterpress and monoprints, in a structure allowing for an intimate reading experience as well as a very wide three-dimensional sculptural object. This book explores ideas about the perception of the world beyond one's own personal experience.

0478 **Breathe** (9 x 8¾ x 5 in [22.5 x 21.9 x 12.5 cm]): A response to "The Flower Soul," a poem by Imogen Brashear Oakley. Two adjacent concertinas leading to the poem hidden behind a relief printed vellum curtain. The book is intaglio, relief, and letterpress printed and housed in a paste paper wrapper.

0479, 0480, 0481 **How Books Work** (4 x 6 in [10 x 15 cm]): Original text and photography, offset printed and presented in a folded enclosure. This book explores ideas about the complexity of the book form itself. Collaboration between a letterpress artist with a love of experimental book structure, and a creator of photographic offset-printed artists' books.

0482, 0483 **Ephemera** (10 x 6 in [25 x 15 cm]): Original wood cut illustrations and letterpress printed poem by Robert Pinksy on Japanese Nishinoushi kozo paper, accordion binding with gatefold, with a goat skin spine.

0484 **Herakles and the Eurystheusian Twelve-Step Program** (11¼ x 6¾ x 1½ in [28.1 x 16.9 x 3.8 cm]): Letterpress printed illustrations by Peggy Gotthold and text by Lawrence G. Van Velzer. Linen cover.

0485, 0486 **Air, Water, Oil** (8¼ x 10½ in [20.6 x 26.3 cm]): Original text and illustrations utilitizing woodcut, photopolymer plates, and hand-set type, printed on Japanese Nishinouchi kozo paper and other mixed media. Cover of black linen dyed Cave cover paper, housed in a silk-covered box.

0487 **One Second of Time** (9 x 9 x 2 in [22.5 x 22.5 x 5.0 cm]): Original text formatted like a seismograph chart, with original mono-prints combined digitally with found earthquake damage imagery and printed with archival inkjet inks.

0488 **The Caretaker** (6 x 8¼ in [15.0 x 20.6 cm]): Double-sided accordion with images from original photographs secreted in a four-fold fabric print wrapper.

0489, 0490 **Conundrum** (6 x 4¼ x ⅜ in [15.0 x 10.6 x 0.9 cm]): Digital inkjet print on rag paper with paper-wrapped hard covers.

0491, 0492 **Visit Wonderland** (1½ x 2 x 1 in [3.8 x 5.0 x 2.5 cm]): Original transfer prints and drawings, with hand-painted watercoloring on tea-dyed Rives BFK and hand-stitched vintage fabric, in milk-painted wood covers.

0493, 0494 **Exquisite** (4¾ x 13¼ x ⅜ in [11.9 x 33.1 x 0.9 cm]): Offset lithography with silk-wrapped hard covers.

0495 **Pandora's Box** (5 x 5 x 5 in [12.5 x 12.5 x 12.5 cm]): Original pen and ink illustrations housed in a corrugated paper-cover box, referencing that even though evils have been released, hope remains.

0496 **Musings: A Tribute to Those Who Sew** (4 x 5 x ½ in [10.0 x 12.5 x 1.3 cm]): Covers made from varied antique and modern hand-stitched lace with hand-stitched embroidery; original text letterpress printed on Rives lightweight paper.

0497, 0498 **LandForms/topographical thinking** (5½ x 9½ x ½ in [13.8 x 23.8 x 1.3 cm]): Original color etching and aquatint, original letterpress text on Somerset Velvet. Cover of Japanese bookcloth over bookboard.

0499, 0500 **Hari-Kuyo, One** (4½ x 5½ x ¾ in [11.3 x 13.8 x 1.9 cm]): Blind embossed cover with linen twist button closure, original solar-plate chine colle etchings and original printed text on rice paper as a familial reference to the Hari-Kuyo broken needle ceremony.

0501, 0502 **Silent Butterflies** (7 x 6½ in [17.5 x 16.3 cm]): Accordion fold book in the round, screen prints on Lokta paper with embroidery.

0503, 0504 **Soap Opera II** (10¾ x 8 x ½ in [26.9 x 20.0 x 1.3 cm]): Digitally manipulated scanned soap ends and stenciled and drawn original illustrations. Inkjet printed on UV ultra paper.

0505 **Awkward** (1 x 3 x ½ in [2.5 x 7.5 x 1.3 cm]): Original letterpress printed text and machine stiching onto paper.

0506 **Tutti E Due** (19 x 7 in [47.5 x 17.5 cm]): Original poem (Italian translation by Al Rubottom) letterpress printed in an accordion-fold-like structure, and featuring hand-painted images.

0507, 0508 **Army Cats** (11 x 13 x ¼ in [27.5 x 32.5 x 0.6 cm]): Flexagon structure with original hand-colored drawings, stencils, and gouache with laser printed text by Tom Sleigh on dyed Eames paper and mylar.

0509, 0510 **La Table de Cuisine** (3 x 1½ x 2¾ in [7.5 x 3.8 x 6.9 cm]): Inkjet printed original text housed in a painted cardboard table.

0511, 0512 **Misremembered Deities: a guide to the small gods of urban life** (3⅝ x 3⅝ x ⅜ in [9.1 x 9.1 x 0.9 cm]): One page

T-cut folded structure of original offset printed text and illustrations on Mohawk Superfine text weight paper.

0513, 0514 **Soirée Dans Le Jardin** (5 x 6 x 3 in [12.5 15.0 x 7.5 cm]): Sewn paper and fabric collage pages with polymer clay covers and handmade polymer clay flowers blossoms.

0515, 0516 **Candide, or Optimism** (7⅜ x 12½ x ½ in [18.4 x 31.3 x 1.3 cm]): Gate-fold accordion based on text by Voltaire, with original screen printed images.

0517 **Two-dollar Dogs** (3 x 5 in [7.5 x 12.5 cm]): Original text and illustrations letterpress printed with photopolymer plates on Somerset paper. Printed hard cover and a handmade paper wrapper.

0518, 0519 **How to Distinguish Scents** (7 x 5 x ½ in [17.5 x 12.5 x 1.3 cm]): Original text, solar plate prints, and watercolors on Rives BFK, sewn into a meandering book with waxed thread.

0520 **Tree Structures** (7½ x 10½ x 1¼ in [18.8 x 26.3 x 3.1 cm]): Original collage on artist's handmade paper, housed in a clamshell box.

0521, 0522 **One Sun—One Apple—One Day** (12 x 8½ x ½ in [30.0 x 21.3 x 1.3 cm]): Unique book of Van Dyke Brown silver-sun prints of the earth (an apple) over the course of one day, with letterpress printed type.

0523, 0524 **Sayings of the Blind** (6 x 4 x ⅛ in [15.0 x 10.0 x 0.3 cm]): Map-fold featuring text by William Stafford letterpress printed from polymer plates on Suminagashi made by Yukari Hayashida, with a Ca L'Oliver handmade paper sleeve.

0525 **Pockets** (8½ x 7½ x 4½ in [21.3 x 18.8 x 11.3 cm]): Found blue jean pockets filled with archival inkjet printed photos of the pocket contents of varied people, along with a list written by each person describing the contents.

0526, 0527 **G Is for Gluttony** (6 x 4½ x ¼ in [15.0 x 11.3 x 0.6 cm]): Original text and illustrations, offset printed on coated commercial paper.

0528, 0529, 0530 **Almanac** (5⅕ x 4⅖ x 1⅕ in [13.0 x 11.0 x 3.0 cm]): Cover made from book board with handmade cotton/linden bast momigami, handmade cotton paper with various plant fibres, inkjet prints of original text, and scanned original collages in the interior. Twined binding with gatefold.

0531 **Passage** (6¼ x 5¼ x ½ in [15.6 x 13.1 x 1.3 cm]): Original Polaroid transfers adhered to fabric, transferred original inkjet printed text, and pulp paper cover.

0532, 0533 **Ice Cream Man** (6½ x 2½ x ¾ in [16.3 x 6.3 x 1.9 cm]): Accordion-fold book of letterpress-printed original text and illustrations with popsicle stick base. Letterpress printed wrapper.

0534 **Compendium** (2½ x 8¼ x 4½ in [6.3 x 20.6 x 11.3 cm]): Extended accordion book of digitally printed text on archival Somerset Velvet, hand-embossed pewter insert on housing, full collection of 1982 state flower and bird commemorative stamps adhered to concertina panels.

0535, 0536 **Spoken** (8 x 5½ x 1 in [20.0 13.8 x 2.5 cm]): Laser printed original text on Kitakata and Arches Text Wove papers with a plexiglass cover accented with embroidery floss.

0537 **Wishing to Unwind** (4 x 4 x ¼ in [10.0 x 10.0 x 0.6 cm]): Accordion book of original letterpress prints and a poem, hand-bound and printed by the artist, expressing a simple wish to relax and rest in the moment.

0538 **Ordinary Heroes** (4½ x 3 x 1 in [11.3 7.5 x 2.5 cm]): Original drawings and text in a compound accordion-fold from a single sheet of confetti text weight paper, housed in a cardstock box.

0539 **The Evolution of the Chinese Character for Woman 1** (2¼ x 1¾ x ¾ in [5.6 4.4 x 1.9 cm]): Original monoprint on Rives BFK housed in a vintage silk-covered box with bone clasp.

0540, 0541, 0542 **The Heart Wants What It Wants** (6 x 6 in [15 x 15 cm]): Boustrophedon structure with original letterpress printed reduction woodcut illustrations and original text and cover images letterpress-printed with photopolymer plates. Hard cover with a clamshell box.

0543 **Circadian Rhythm** (10 x 5½ x 2½ in [25.0 13.8 x 6.3 cm]): Watercolor stained paper with caterpillar stitching, image transfers and graphite drawing with covers of found metal and stained wood.

0544, 0545 **Alphabet Ancestors** (5¼ x 4¼ x 1 in [13.1 x 10.6 x 2.5 cm]): Four-fold wrapper of bark paper and deerskin with a strap closure, three enclosed books casein-painted with abstract symbols and letters, and a fourth book with a printed essay.

0546, 0547 **What Would Gutenberg Think Now?** (8½ x 2¾ x 2 in [21.3 x 6.9 x 5.0 cm]): Digitally printed text, with inserts of TXT messages.

0548 **The Wine** (2 x 1 x 1 in [5.0 x 2.5 x 2.5 cm]): Original black ink and watercolor artwork, color-photocopied, with text from *The Odyssey* by Homer, on Peter Thomas' handmade paper. Cork cover.

0549 **It Didn't Just Happen** (9 x 6½ in [22.5 x 16.3 cm]): Original letterpress printed text and illustrations on Mohawk superfine paper and Canford cover paper.

0550, 0551 **The Wedding Plans** (2¼ x 2¼ x 1 in [5.6 x 5.6 x 2.5 cm]): Original text, hand-set and letterpress printed by the artist on handmade cotton paper.

0552, 0553 **Where Is My Home?** (10 x 6½ x ¾ in [25.0 x 16.3 x 1.9 cm]): Original text and illustrations telling the tale of finding Smokey the dog, printed in off-set lithography on Strathmore cover paper; blind embossed Japanese silk bookcloth cover.

0554, 0555 **Creep** (5½ x 3½ x ¼ in [13.8 x 8.8 x 0.6 cm]): Letterpress printed with hand-set type and original linoleum cut illustrations on French Dur-O-Tone Steel Grey paper; explores decay and chaos.

0556 **Navigation** (9½ x 5¾ x 1¼ in [23.8 x 14.4 x 3.1 cm]): Letterpress printed and colored paper with hand-cut holes creating constellations based on city names based on reoccurences of city names throughout the country, bound in cloth-covered boards.

0557, 0558 **Balada Para Un Loco II (Song for a Madman II)** (3¾ x 3¾ x ¾ in [9.4 x 9.4 x 1.9 cm]): Drawn, painted and collaged images inspired by the lyrics by Horacio Ferrer for the tango "Balada Para Un Loco." Edition of 75.

0559 **A Florentine Alphabet** (5¾ x 5¾ x ⅞ in [14.4 x 14.4 x 2.2 cm]): An abecedary structured on the Italian alphabet. Modified accordion-fold with original archival inkjet text and images on heavy-weight Rives paper, cover of silk screened paper and corrugated paper.

0560 **Sonnet** (6¼ x 6¼ x 1¼ in [15.6 15.6 x 3.1 cm]): Circular accordion structure featuring a digitally typeset Sonnet by William Shakespeare and a transferred portrait engraving by Martin Droeshout (1623).

0561, 0562, 0563 **Genesis 32.29** (12 x 12¾ x ¾ in [30.0 x 31.9 x 1.9 cm]): Original colored woodcuts and letterpress printed text from the Bible.

0564, 0565 **A Village Dance** (6½ x 6½ x ¾ in [16.3 x 16.3 x 1.9 cm]): Original papercuts on cardstock bound on accordion folds; cover with handmade bookcloth.

0566, 0567 **How Time Flies** (6 x 3 x ⅝ in [15.0 x 7.5 x 1.6 cm]): Folded and hand-stitched found calendar pages with machine-stitched thread birds.

0568, 0569 **Calliope, Muse of Epic Poetry** (9 x 3⅓ x 3 in [22.5 x 8.3 x 7.5 cm]): Original calligraphy of text from Homer's *Iliad* on paste paper with inks, acrylics, and pastels. Archival black board and copper foil.

0570, 057-1 **Grimoire** (16 x 5 x 1½ in [40.0 x 12.5 x 3.8 cm]): Accordion fold structure with fold out pages containing original text, cut out by hand, with covers of cardboard relief with pewter wax.

0572, 0573 **Shattered in the Shaky City** (9½ x 4¼ x 1 in [23.8 x 10.6 x 2.5 cm]): Digitally manipulated original photographs and gouache painting, with a cover of Japanese paper with on-laid text.

0574, 0575 **Aftermath** (9½ x 7 in [23.8 x 17.5 cm]): Original Sumi ink wash on artist-made abaca paper with gold- and silver-leafed cover, and linen cording. Portrait of tornado downed trees on artist's Missouri land.

0576 **To Unknown Artists** (8 x 8 x 2 in [20.0 x 20.0 x 5.0 cm]): A tribute to ancient rock artists, with original linocuts, batik, and pulp painting on abaca, flax, and thistle with walnut stain and wax in French door, accordion, and tunnel structures.

0577 **Torn Clouds & Cranes** (4 x 5½ x ¾ in [10.0 x 13.8 x 1.9 cm]): Layered and stitched accordion fold of original pencil drawings on vellum with pastel paper. Polymer clay covers with photo transfers.

0578, 0579 **Five Days at Carnarvon Gorge** (12 x 4 x 1 in [30.0 x 10.0 x 2.5 cm]): Hand-spun papers, colored by rubbing onto surfaces in the Carnarvon Gorge, woven into Australian linen thread warps. Used collograph plate cover.

0580, 0581 **Christmas Eve Day** (10 x 10 x ½ in [25.0 x 25.0 x 1.3 cm]): Photocopy and photocopy transfer of handwritten original text on handmade abaca, gampi, and kozo paper with linen thread.

0582, 0583 **roll & steep turn** (8 x 5 x ½ in [20.0 x 12.5 x 1.3 cm]): Original etching with pastel and pencil on BFK Rives.

0584, 0585, 0586 **La Cité des Animaux** (9 x 8½ x ¾ in [22.5 x 21.3 x 1.9 cm]): Original collages utilizing images from A. Seba's *Naturalium Thesauri* and other antique works. Cover of bookcloth-covered boards with ornament of air-dry clay and repurposed metal locket with added collage images.

0587, 0588 **Do Not Disturb** (7 x 3 x 1 in [17.5 x 7.5 x 2.5 cm]): Acrylic board accordion book made with alcohol inks, photocopied transparencies, lace, and other ephemera. Unique linen tape binding structure designed by the artist.

0589, 0590 **Travels with the Geisha** (8½ x 8½ x ⅞ in [21.3 x 21.3 x 2.2 cm]): Original collage utilizing vintage Japanese postcards and antique etchings with vintage travel ephemera tucked into cover pockets. Cover of paper-covered boards.

0591, 0592 **Layers of New Mexico** (5¼ x 5½ x 2½ in [13.1 x 13.8 x 6.3 cm]): Original linoprints, collographs, and embossing with found objects.

0593, 0594, 0595 **Citizen Hydra** (10 x 9¼ x ½ in [25.0 x 23.1 x 1.3 cm]): Original text and artwork in wood cut prints, screen prints, and hand-stamping on handmade cotton rag. Cover of handmade denim paper over boards, with hand-stamping and handmade paper of cotton rag and flags.

0596 **Magical NatureScapes** (6 x 8½ in [15.2 x 21.6 cm]): Combines vintage 3-D concept with modern technology. Scenic 3-D photos, removable or held in a folded spine with mini pockets, a text signature with 3-D history, 3-D glasses, cover with magnetic closure.

0597, 0598 **Neo Emblemata Nova** (3 x 3 x 3 in [7.5 x 7.5 x 7.5 cm]): Art and text from Emblemata Nova, aka Atalanta Fugiens, by Michael Maier assembled into a Möbius strip accordion book. Offset printed, wire edge binding with brass and stainless steel hinges. Techniques include laser welding, paint spattering, and soldering.

0599, 0600 **Applicant** (4½ x 8 x 1 in [11.3 x 20.0 x 2.5 cm]): Original color pencil drawing with collages, text, and rubber stamps. Leather with on-lay cover.

0601, 0602, 0603 **Human Mannerisms** (5 x 4 x ¼ in [12.5 x 10.0 x 0.6 cm]): Original artwork digitally printed on paper.

0604 **Janae Learns About Color** (8¼ x 10½ x ¾ in [20.6 x 26.3 x 1.9 cm]): Pulp-painted cotton and abaca paper made by the artist, housed in a clamshell box.

0605, 0606 **Show** (4 ¾ x 4 ¾ x ½ in [11.9 x 11.9 x 1.3 cm]): Unique book of collaged woodcut, serigraph, and intaglio prints with drawing, about the performer and the audience.

0607 **In Praise of the Art of Cooking** (12 x 7 x 1 in [30.0 x 17.5 x 2.5 cm]): Cover of plastic cutting boards with original engravings and ink with piano hinges. Interior of archival inkjet prints of original photography and text on Hahnemühle injet paper.

0608 **Spring Whispers** (7½ x 3¼ x 1 in [18.8 x 8.1 x 2.5 cm]): Monotypes pulled on an etching press with rubber-based inks, suminagashi on washi, folded and attached, and machine stitching.

0609, 0610 **Team Evil + High Anxiety** (6⅞ x 4¾ x ⅛ in [17.2 x 11.9 x 0.3 cm]): Instant book, which turns inside-out to be two books, which show through the semi-translucent, vintage handmade Bodleian paper. Original linocut illustrations and hand-set metal type.

0611 **INFLATION: A Biased View** (5 x 2½ x 2¾ in [12.5 x 6.3 x 6.9 cm]): Vintage bias tape packets arranged in ascending prices from 8¢ to $2.35 showing inflation over time, attached to accordion fold binding with endpapers of original collages.

0612 **Pancakes!** (1¼ x 1¼ x ½ in [3.1 x 3.1 x 1.3 cm]): Laser prints of original watercolors with button covers.

0613, 0614 **In Forests, Volume XXIII: Natural History** (9½ x 8¾ x ¾ in [23.8 x 21.9 x 1.9 cm]): Case-bound accordion-fold book of seven folios with imagery front and back and matching slip case. Watercolor, gouache, ink, colored pencil, pastel, gold, pollen, and ash on 260 lb. Arches hotpress watercolor paper. Paste-painted Tyvek and rayon bookcloth-covered boards and case.

0615, 0616 **Le Meschere della Commedia dell'Art** (2½ x 9½ x 1¾ in [6.3 x 23.8 x 4.4 cm]): Illustrations by Maurice Sand printed in wax ink, then transferred onto Modigliani paper, with inkjet printed text. Watercolor painted pages sewn into a sextuple accordion structure, housed in a clamshell box.

0617, 0618 **Red Altar** (12 x 11½ x ½ in [30.0 x 28.8 x 1.3 cm]): Monotypes pulled on an etching press with rubber-based inks, orizomegami with Sumi ink, and machine stitching.

0619, 0620 **Archetypal Illuminations** (7¾ x 6⅛ x 1 in [19.4 x 15.3 x 2.5 cm]): Seven original paper collage panels, with a 2 x 2 inch (5 x 5 cm) book of text held to cover by magnets.

0621 **Sweet Grass: My Place** (10 x 3½ x 1 in [25.0 x 8.8 x 2.5 cm]): Original text letterpress printed with polymer plates on Sekishi paper with walnut ink, prairie grass.

0622, 0623 **Rumor of Wars** (6 x 4½ x 1½ in [15.0 x 11.3 x 3.8 cm]): Three solid oak panels attached with antique window hinges. Text from Matthew 24:6-7 collaged with found text and images, illustrating the futility of man's existence.

0624, 0625 **Busy as a Bee** (3½ x 3 x ½ in [8.8 x 7.5 x 1.3 cm]): Hexagon book of original digital images covering boards, with brass charm and ribbon.

0626, 0627 **Perplexed** (5¾ x 5¼ x ⅞ in [14.4 x 13.1 x 2.2 cm]): Circle accordion of original text and illustrations in acrylic artists' ink.

0628, 0629 **Counting with Tools** (2¾ x 2¼ x ½ in [6.9 x 5.6 x 1.3 cm]): Original black ink and watercolor artwork and text, color photocopied on Peter Thomas' handmade paper. Dowel hinge spine of nail hardware.

0630, 0631 **Hit the Road, Jack** (14 x 6 in [35.0 x 15.0 cm]): Found toy truck housing an accordion book of original collaged pages that include quotes about travel. "A good traveler has no fixed plans and is not intent on arriving." — Lao Tzu

0632, 0633 **Possessed by the Furies** (2½ x 6½ x 7½ in [6.3 x 16.3 x 18.8 cm]): Original etchings, aquatints, and blind embossing drawn on copper by the artist, and printed by Barbara Madsen on Hahnemühle Biblio paper. Letterpress printing and binding by Jana Pullman of Western Slope Press. Custom handmade wooden box by John Studebaker with enamel inlay by artist.

0634, 0635, 0636 **Oneiro** (5 x 4¾ x 3½ in [12.5 x 11.9 x 8.8 cm]): Pinhole camera cover created from a found tin box. Wire rod and hinge binding of original pinhole photography and original text.

0637 **The Real Accordion Book** (13 x 15 x 6 in [32.5 x 37.5 x 15.0 cm]): Binding is a real accordion with bellows slit to make accordion folding pages. Text is handwritten, a history of the accordion, with hand-colored photographs printed on Peter's handmade paper.

0638, 0639 **6 metri e 20 di omologazione (6 meters and 20 Official Approvals)** (4 x 18 x 4 in [10.0 x 45.0 x 10.0 cm]): Scroll book with stencil printing and a felt cover.

0640, 0641 **Knight's Prayer** (16 x 2 x 2 in [40 x 5 x 5 cm]): Original drawing in acrylic ink on goatskin and parchment.

0642, 0643 **Rites Rituals Ruminations—Faces That Speak** (32½ x 6½ x 4⅞ in [81.3 x 16.3 x 12.2 cm]): C & C Press artists' book featuring photography by Stephen Verona, offset printed on French Smart White paper, presented in a handmade box using book cloth, binder's board, digital and letterpress type.

0644, 0645 **Phrenology Book** (4 x 5 x 1 in [10.0 x 12.5 x 2.5 cm]): Loose pages of archival inkjet prints on dress pattern paper, vintage found images and original photographs, housed in a handmade box covered with vintage dress pattern paper, silk ribbon, and ivory buttons.

0646 **Alphabet** (5 x 5 x 2 in [12.5 x 12.5 x 5.0 cm]): Scroll book of found antique nails sewn on cotton, mounted on found wooden spools embellished with oxidized copper.

0647, 0648 **Corsay and Blum** (10 x 9 x 5 in [25.0 x 22.5 x 12.5 cm]): Handmade paper and mixed media, cover of handmade pigmented gampi and plastic.

0649, 0650, 0651 **Know Good & Evil** (10 x 4 x 4 in [25.0 x 10.0 x 10.0 cm]): Cliff Notes on the Old Testament, altered to resemble the dead sea scrolls. Genesis 3:22 runs both sides the length of the scroll, quoted in Hebrew and English. Distressed leather cover, aged and altered, gel medium transfers of original illustrations, found images and text cut from various publications.

0652, 0653 **Measuring Up** (6 x 6 x 3 in [15.0 x 15.0 x 7.5 cm]): Poetry by Liam Rector and original illustrations printed with aluminium and smart plate lithography and text transfer techniques onto Moriki paper.

0654 **A Perfect Love** (4 x 4 x ⅝ in [10.0 x 10.0 x 1.6 cm]): Original text incised into plastic sheets, housed in bronze.

0655 **Oil Slick Flag** (5¾ x 15½ x ¾ in [14.4 x 38.8 x 1.9 cm]): Tibetan-style book of unbound pages with Polaroid transfers from original photos on artist's handmade paper; Crisco mixed with powdered graphite between adhered vellum sheets. Housed between book board covers with a Tyvek wrapping cloth.

0656 **My Kaddish** (2¼ x 1¼ x ⅞ in [5.6 x 3.1 x 2.2 cm]): Original calligraphy and drawings in ink, graphite, and watercolor on Japanese rice paper, with polymer clay panels (with transferred photocopy images of original drawings and photographs) laminated between pieces of rice paper. Polymer clay box.

0657, 0658 **September 11, 2001 Harvest** (10 x 8½ x 1¾ in [25.0 x 21.3 x 4.4 cm]): Tibetan-style book of unbound pages of inkjet printed text, collaged black and white photographs on glasseine, colored copies of news images on Japanese handmade paper, and Polaroid transfers on artist's handmade paper. Quotes from Pablo Neruda, Barbara Lee, The Dalai Lama, Uri Avnery, Thich Nhat Hahn, and Yehuda Amichai. Housed in a bookboard box treated with powdered graphite in solution.

0659, 0660 **Copper Stone Portfolio** (1¼ x 1 x ⅖ in [3.1 x 2.5 x 1.1 cm]): Unique portfolio made from found pieces of copper hinged with paper, holding original watercolor and pencil illustrations of tiny rocks. All housed in a box made from folded copper sheets with engraving.

0661, 0662 **Bernoulli Equation for Unsteady Potential Flow** (2½ x 7¾ x 1¾ in [6.3 x 19.4 x 4.4 cm]): Palm leaf book (digital pigment prints from original photographs) with action that mimics the behavior of a moving body of water.

0663, 0664, 0665 **The McGinley Paper Company Sample Book of Faults** (6 x 9 x ¼ in [15.0 x 22.5 x 0.6 cm]): Letterpress printed anonymous "faults" submitted by survey responders. Hand-carved woodcut prints based on vintage textile designs.

0666, 0667 **Fish Stories** (3⅕ x 9 x 2 in [8.0 x 22.5 x 5.0 cm]): Up-cycled materials including a jello mold holding hand-painted papers collaged onto wood. Artist's original funny fish poem witten for her son. Inkjet printed text.

0668, 0669 **5 Quotes on a Heartbeat!** (2 x 15 in [5.0 x 37.5 cm]): Original illustrations with quotations about love, color printed and wrapped around a clothespin.

0670, 0671 **Nautilus Scroll Book #2** (3¼ x 4½ x 3½ in [8.1 x 11.3 x 8.8 cm]): Original haiku, handwritten on the back of specialty acrylic-over-marbled paper, housed in cut, bent, glued, and covered bookboard.

0672, 0673, 0674 **REP-HAIR-ATION** (16 x 21 x 1½ in [40.0 x 52.5 x 3.8 cm]): Portfolio book of fifteen prints by Diane Jacobs, housed in boxes made by Rachel Wiecking. Pages include handmade cotton paper by Helen Hiebert, mulberry paper, Frankfurt paper, felt, with handset letterpress text. Various illustration techniques include etching, collograph, woodblock, five color reduction linoleum cut, photo engravings, gocco printed dollar bill, and kumihimo (Japanese braiding of human hair).

0675 **Love Notes** (2½ x 3½ x 1 in [6.3 x 8.8 x 2.5 cm]): Letterpress printing from photopolymer plates and hand-set type on Crane Lettra paper inspired by notes the artist and his wife left for each other.

0676 **Delusion** (10 x 13 x 2 in [25.0 x 32.5 x 5.0 cm]): Original silk screen in enamel on aluminum with metal leaf.

0677, 0678 **The Mystical Quality of Handiwork** (2¾ x 2 x ¾ in [6.9 x 5.0 x 1.9 cm]): Binding is leather, scroll frame is wood with brass cranks. Text by Victor Hammer was letterpress printed (using Hammer's original type and his wooden hand press) on Peter's handmade paper. A piece of Hammer's type is affixed inside the front cover.

0679, 0680 **The Third Letter** (1 x ½ x ½ in [2.5 x 1.3 x 1.3 cm]): Original text (calligraphy by Minoru Sasaki), printed with resin letterpress plate.

0681, 0682 **For Now** (12 x 9½ x ¾ in [30.0 x 23.8 x 1.9 cm]): Original aquatints and letterpress printing on paper and cloth, French loose leaf in box.

0683 **The Bird Speaks** (6⅛ x 4½ x 5⅛ in [15.3 x 11.3 x 12.8 cm]): Vintage postcards altered with found text and images bound in a handmade portfolio case created from letterpressed abaca and cotton handmade paper, binder's board, and Asahi bookcloth.

0684 **My Great-Grandmother's Clothesline** (12 x 36 in [30.0 x 90.0 cm]): Text from artist's grandmother's letters to her daughter silk screened onto vintage handkerchiefs.

0685, 0686, 0687 **Language Möbius** (5½ x 10 x 2½ in [13.8 x 25.0 x 6.3 cm]): Original text in English and Korean, letterpress printed from polymer plates on Somerset paper, twisted into möbius strips, illustrating artist's mental process in carrying on a conversation in English. Housed in handmade Jacob's Ladder box.

0688 **El Mar** (7 x 1 x 1 in [17.5 x 2.5 x 2.5 cm]): Original silk screen and woodcut prints on Cave paper.

0689 **No hay respuestas aquí (There Are No Answers Here)** (55 x 50 x 3 in [137.5 x 125.0 x 7.5 cm]): Scroll with moveable folds, original text and drawings on graph paper with pencil, dry pigment, acrylic paint and medium, wax, and thread.

0690, 0691 **California Dreaming** (3 x 6 x 3 in [7.5 x 15 x 7.5 cm]): The lyrics to Jan and Dean's "Surf City" (I got a '34 wagon and we call it a woodie...) are printed on a scroll, with a hand-painted photo collage of surf and woodie images on the back. The scroll turns on a brass crank mechanism mounted inside a toy "woodie". Title page glued to wooden surfboard.

0692, 0693 **In Celebration of Two** (6¼ x 19¾ x ¾ in [15.6 x 49.4 x 1.9 cm]): A palm-leaf-inspired binding with birch bark covers, closure with silk twine cords. Text and illustration by the artist, with original brush lettering and collage.

0694 **BEAUT.E(CODE)** (3¼ x 7¼ x ½ in [8.1 x 18.1 x 1.3 cm]): Text from interviews with software developers conducted and edited by the artist, entered on computer punch cards with a keypunch machine. Custom-printed rubber band.

0695, 0696 **Prayers for Fallen Trees** (8 x 2 x 1½ in [20.0 x 5.0 x 3.8 cm]): Palm leaf book with ink and collage on handmade paper.

0697 **The Odd Volumes of Ruby B.**: Collection of books with exposed spine bindings made from book pages, fabric, and photographs stitched into collages.

0698, 0699 **The Odd Volumes of Ruby B., No. 17** (8½ x 7 x 1 in [21.3 x 17.5 x 2.5 cm]): Longstitch-bound volume of book pages with fabric, paper, and photographs stitched into collages.

0700, 0701 **Felix' Notebooks**: Collection of re-bound altered books with exposed spine bindings, each line of the book's text stitched through in red thread.

0702, 0703 **Wrapped Words** (6 x 4½ x 4 in [15.0 x 11.3 x 10.0 cm]): Discarded pages of *The Handmaid's Tale* by Margaret Atwood, with machine stitching and Greek coptic binding, created for a Banned Book exhibit.

0704, 0705 **The Gray Box** (7¼ x 7 ¼ x 4 in [18.1 x 18.1 x 10.0 cm]): Text from *The Picture of Dorian Gray* by Oscar Wilde, and other original text archival inkjet printed on Rives BFK with covers of mat board and commercial paper. Clip art and stockphotos digitally manipulated by artist. Housed in box with silk bookcloth and purchased paper roses and metal legs.

0706 **Floating Memories** (45 x 10 feet per panel [13.7 x 3.0 m]): Public art story-telling installation of cut Tyvek.

0707, 0708 **All Fifty-two Cards** (40 x 20 x 4 in [100.0 x 50.0 x 10.0 cm]): Altered book on how to play bridge suspended between steel beams.

0709, 0710, 0711, 0712, 0713, 0714 **The Restless Sleeper**: A constructed box filled with music, flip books, and accordion books featuring original text and illustrations created with techniques including encaustic wax painting, gold foil stamping, and embroidery.

0715, 0716 **Biedermeier: Modern Before Its Time** (19 x 10 x 4 in [47.5 x 25.0 x 10.0 cm]): Digitally printed original miniature books housed in a fabricated and painted museum board "Biedermeier" cabinet. Books bound in silk Japanese book cloth.

0717, 0718 **Art Deco: Bold & Sassy** (10½ x 9 x 2½ in [26.3 x 22.5 x 6.3 cm]): Acrylic and ink images (in the style of Tamara de Lempicka) on handmade paper housed in an Art Deco style sideboard made from museum board and painted Japanese book cloth.

0719, 0720, 0721 **Direction of the Road** (14¾ x 12¾ x 2 in [36.9 x 31.9 x 5.0 cm]): Letterpress printed illustrations by Aaron Johnson and text by Ursula K. LeGuin, Japanese cloth cover.

0722, 0723, 0724 **Small Museum of Nature and Industry** (2 x 2 x 2½ in [5.0 x 5.0 x 6.3 cm]): Removable puzzle blocks in a collaged book of slate, birch plywood, basswood, Tyvek, metals, and mirror.

0725, 0726 **Life Stories of Dying Penitents** (7 x 5 x 1½ in [17.5 x 12.5 x 3.8 cm]): Artist-edited anonymous nineteenth-century text, found book containing collage and assemblage incorporating gouache, etched metal, and mirror.

0727 **Crested** (14 x 7 x 2½ in [35.0 x 17.5 x 6.3 cm]): Carved and painted spalted maple, yew, mica, fossils, handmade paper, milk paint, fossilized insect amber, and other found objects. Ethiopian and Coptic bindings.

0728, 0729 **Things I Have Eaten** (10 x 22 x 9 in [25.0 x 55.0 x 22.5 cm]): Handmade papier-mâché dog on wheels holding a codex of original gouache and graphite illustrations and original typewritten text on Rives BFK paper.

0730 C**onfessions of a Small Dog** (7 x 10 x 6 in [17.5 x 25.0 x 15.0 cm]): Handmade papier-mâché dog with pencil leg with a codex of original gouache and graphite illustrations and typewritten text on Rives BFK paper.

0731 **Rat Race** (12 x 19 x 8 in [30.0 x 47.5 x 20.0 cm]): Original calligraphy and hand-stitching with installation pieces including a hamster wheel, rubber rat, and hardware.

0732 **Jewel Sonnets** (4 x 4 x 4 in [10.0 x 10.0 x 10.0 cm]): Text by William Shakespeare, handwritten by the artist on leather parchment pages with natural pearls on a leather cord.

0733, 0734 **Reflecting Light** (7 x 5 in [17.5 x 12.5 cm]): Encaustic, industrial, and combed wax vessel featuring inspirational quotations reflected through the wax. Organza fabric book accompanies sculpture.

0735 **Boat of Words** (7 x 4 x 28 in [17.5 x 10.0 x 70.0 cm]): Original handwritten text and handcut rubber stamps with transluscent layers of Lokta paper and dried blades of grass.

0736 **Cubric of Curios** (4 x 4 x 4 in [10.0 x 10.0 x 10.0 cm]): Eight hinged cubes with original digital images and text on lokta paper on book board; with mica, artifacts, and bells.

0737, 0738 **Hamlet** (11 x 5 x 5 in [27.5 x 12.5 x 12.5 cm]): Shakespeare's *Hamlet* in a miniature historical binding, housed in a sculpture of carved and painted wood and plasticine. Computer-generated printing on artist's handmade paper.

0739, 0740, 0741 **Recipes for Kneeling (version 1)** (2 x 6 x 9 in [5.0 x 15.0 x 22.5 cm]): Installation of twelve illuminated books exploring language, meaning, and the spirit, featuring original text, collages, and drawings.

0742 **Deception** (5 x 7 x ¼ in [12.5 x 17.5 x 0.6 cm]): Original silk screen and painting on aluminum sheets, mounted on edge to the wall.

0743, 0744, 0745 **My Boat Is So Small, The Ocean So Large** (120 x 96 x 12 in [300 x 240 x 30 cm]): Installation of original pencil and graphite drawings, inkjet prints, hand-constructed boat models, with steel, fiberglass cloth, and other materials.

0746, 0747 **Palimpsesto** (30 x 30 feet [9.1 x 9.1 m]): Unique book with original calligraphy in Sumi ink on kraft paper.

0748, 0749 **Tree House** (14½ x 16½ x 6 in [36.3 x 41.3 x 15.0 cm]): Mixed mouldmade and decorative papers, bookcloth, housed in a handmade wood sculpture.

0750, 0751 **Heart to Heart Talk** (12 x 12 x 12 in [30.0 x 30.0 x 30.0 cm]): Book made of wood, acrylic paint, and rubber stamps. Read by turning center wheel (text block) and sharing between two readers. Words make a sound as the wheel turns.

0752 **From One Place to Another** (11 x 16 x 9½ in [27.5 x 40.0 x 23.8 cm]): Handmade box with original digital illustrations housing a book with simplified binding containing original images and poems printed on papers and Yupo synthetic paper.

0753, 0754 **Fragmented Relations** (12 x 12 x 12 in [30.0 x 30.0 x 30.0 cm]): Rotating/revolving cube structure illustrating the complexity of family relationships. Original oil paintings, digitized and cropped, printed with archival pigments on matte cover paper, varnished and applied to binders board covered with book cloth.

0755 **Alphabook** (3 x 4 in [7.5 x 10.0 cm]): Altered books and hardware.

0756 **The Compleat Enchanter** (6½ x 6 x 1¾ in [16.3 x 15.0 x 4.4 cm]): Altered books and mixed media including acrylic, plaster, hardware, and encaustic.

0757 **Colony 45** (21 x 21 in [52.5 x 52.5 cm]): Forty-five removable hand-bound books with acrylic and watercolor applied in layers on artist's handmade paper.

0758, 0759 **Sound Blocks** (2 x 8½ x 2 in [5.0 x 21.3 x 5.0 cm]): Laser-cut and hand-assembled artist-made cotton paper, housed in a cherry wood box with glass lid.

0760 **Me See How You Do It** (6 x 22½ x 2½ in [15.0 x 56.3 x 6.3 cm]): Stitched book sculpture of discarded book fragments and other objects.

0761, 0762 **Forest Lake** (300 x 8 in [750.0 x 20.0 cm]): Poem by Edith Södergran, handwoven in wool and cotton, with ikat dying and embroidery.

0763 **Japanese Motives** (8 x 6 in [20.0 x 15.0 cm]): Classical Japanese poetry translated into Russian and written in original calligraphy on cast handmade paper. Book is intended to be suspended and shaken by the wind to create rustling in the pages like a tree in a forest.

0764 **Forest Lullaby** (3¼ x 2¼ x ½ in [8.1 x 5.6 x 1.3 cm]): Original two-plate carved and hand-pulled relief print on artist's handmade paper, scanned and combined with text of original poem. Handmade suspended stars, and cover of bookcloth and handmade bead.

0765, 0766 **Nestler** (16 x 13 x 1½ in [40.0 x 32.5 x 3.8 cm]): Text from an early-ninteenth-century family record of births and deaths, indicating that many children were lost at young ages. Red willow and various handmade papers, with crochet, hand stitching, machine sewing, and embroidery, honoring the young souls in limbo.

0767, 0768, 0769 **Unfoldings** (3 x 3 x 3 in [7.5 x 7.5 x 7.5 cm]): A flexicube structure of inkjet prints over linen-hinged wood cubes, unfolding to separate and rejoin photographic images of ancestral Danish sites and handwritten dream text about emigration and diaspora.

0770 **Rolodex: Organize Your Life** (4 x 4½ x 8½ in [10.0 x 11.3 x 21.3 cm]): Collage, drawing, pianting, rubber stamping, screen printing, and journaling on a variety of paper in a Rolodex holder.

0771, 0772 **myTurningPointe** (3 x 3 x 2 in [7.5 x 7.5 x 5.0 cm]): An accordion-fold book that transforms into a tutu, of machine-stitched handmade abaca paper, tulle and pointe shoe ribbon. Original text excerpted from personal journals, printed with archival digital pigments.

0773 **SavedBooks81LesFleurDuMal** (9½ x 14 x 6½ in [23.8 x 35.0 x 16.3 cm]): Recycled book painted with dry pigments, wetted, formed into undulated curls, and dried.

0774, 0775 **Man of Sorrow** (18 x 8 x 8 in [45.0 x 20.0 x 20.0 cm]): Tabletop installation with found carving, glass dome, and codex containing original calligraphy and watercolor.

0776 **A Year on Accabonac Harbor** (8½ x 24 x 4 in [21.3 x 60.0 x 10.0 cm]): Artist's original text and illustration by Carroll B. Cline inkjet printed on pamphlet-bound Somerset Velvet paper.

0777, 0778 **Awakening Beneath the Yoke** (16 x 6 x 6 in [40.0 x 15.0 x 15.0 cm]): Tabletop installation with found carving and codex of altered Bible pages.

0779, 0780 **The Pagoda** (30 x 12 x 12 in [75.0 x 30.0 x 30.0 cm]): Tabletop installation of papier-mâché pagoda, handmade books with original calligraphy and watercolor, and handmade screen and an antique Japanese doll (the storyteller).

0781, 0782 **PodCast** (15 x 31 x 3 in [37.5 x 77.5 x 7.5 cm]): Found organic pods, found text, acrylic paint, chalk, graphite, plexiglass, and steel bolts.

0783, 0784 **Archetypes: Journey to Self** (6 x 6 x 6 in [15.0 x 15.0 x 15.0 cm]): Boxed set of 13 artists' books in codex, star tunnel, and scroll styles. Archival ditigal pigment prints of original photographs, graphics, and text on handmade and other papers and Mylar, with garnets and garnet dust, nickel hands, and other mixed media.

0785, 0786 **Ironstone Book** (6 x 4½ x 4½ in [15 x 11.3 x 11.3 cm]): Hand-bound book of original archival inkjet photos of artist's ironstone collection on watercolor paper. Cover of vintage ironstone watercolor pans bound with cotton and linen, housed in a wood and glass case with dollhouse furniture and mixed media accents.

0787 **Issues of Domesticity** (3 x 3 x 3 in [7.5 x 7.5 x 7.5 cm]): Collection of books with hand-embroidery, Xerox transfers, beading, collage, and found objects with covers of canvas, steel plates, clay. Coptic binding, long-stitch binding, and altered book structures.

0788, 0789 **Pinky Bra** (11 x 23 x 3 in [27.5 x 57.5 x 7.5 cm]): Woven handset letterpress text of derogatory words used against women. This piece makes feminist references to craft, the body, and our misogynist culture.

0790, 0791 **Pumping Iron** (10 x 12 x 7 in [25.0 x 30.0 x 17.5 cm]): Original text letterpress printed with liquid polymer plates onto handmade denim paper, case of fabricated stainless steel.

0792, 0793, 0794 **I Do (I Don't)** (23 x 14 x 14 in [57.5 x 35.0 x 35.0 cm]): Three gameboards featuring letterpress and laser printing, housed in a blind debossed handmade cotton/flax paper wedding cake.

0795 **Music of the World** (9¼ x 7⅝ x 1⅜ in [23.1 x 19.1 x 3.4 cm]): Sealed and carved found book. Excavating images and samples from Music's history.

0796, 0797 **Webster Withdrawn** (11¾ x 16½ x 13¼ in [29.4 x 41.3 x 33.1 cm]): Sealed and carved found book. Illustrating the idea of loss through technology.

0798, 0799 **New Books of Knowledge** (16 x 26½ x 10 in [40.0 x 66.3 x 25.0 cm]): Sealed and carved combined found books.

0800 **7 Hours in a Cave** (9 x 8 x 5 in [22.5 x 20.0 x 12.5 cm]): Artist's cotton paper with abaca pulp paint cast over original rubber mold. Cast pages are partially painted with encaustic and acrylic and bound with waxed linen thread and grommets.

0801, 0802 **A Place to Be** (7½ x 7½ x 9 in [18.8 x 18.8 x 22.5 cm]): Handmade box with original digital illustrations under glass, containing accordion and dos-à-dos bound books of original images and poems inkjet printed on paper and Yupo synthetic paper.

0803 **Fehling's Solution** (9¾ x 8⅓ x 3½ in [24.4 x 20.8 x 8.8 cm]): Original text and flexographic and screen printed illustrations with watercolor hand-tinting. With etched bottle, all encased in a wooden box.

0804, 0805 **Americana** (40½ x 70½ x 2½ in [101.3 x 176.3 x 6.3 cm]): Sealed and carved combined found books. A field of fragmented images throughout history

0806, 0807 **During the War** (6 x 16 x ½ in [15.0 x 40.0 x 1.3 cm]): Hand- and machine-stitched book sculpture of paper, buttons, and thread.

0808, 0809, 0810 **What I Can't Tell You**: Original text letterpress printed and machine-stitched onto ribbon and felt, with vintage spools and thimble, all housed in a vintage sewing box.

0811, 0812 **Fragment: Crozet, approx. 1978-1983** (12 x 10 x 7 in [30.0 x 25.0 x 17.5 cm]): Original text and images, printed on Epson 1280 printer.

0813, 0814 **Blush** (3½ x 4 x 2½ in [8.8 x 10.0 x 6.3 cm]): Book of hand-dyed Kozo with hand-stamped text repeating the word "Transcience." Plexiglass box containing a copy of the I Ching, dyed pink and chopped into confetti. In remembrance of a dear friend, lost to breast cancer.

0815, 0816 **Pages** (70 x 4 x 3 in [175.0 x 10.0 x 7.5 cm]): Images of books, reframed… Original photography inket printed on photo paper with bookcloth, Davey bookboard, and cotton cords.

0817 **Circular Logic** (10 x 11 x 7 in [25.0 27.5 x 17.5 cm]): Rolled dictionary pages and glue inspired by the never-ending circle of definitions.

0818, 0819 **Aircraft**: Altered book installation.

0820, 0821 **Transparent People** (7¾ x 9¾ x 9¾ in [19.4 x 24.4 x 24.4 cm]): Original text, laser printed on transparencies and bound with cardstock to a glass block.

0822 **TWO FALL, FALL TO, FALL TOO, FALL** (8 x 5½ x ¼ in [20.0 x 13.8 x 0.6 cm]): Record of concurrent 9/11 events (terrorist attacks and personal eye surgery), abstract nonverbal response, visual poem narrative, made from an altered blank hardcover book with torn papers and original narrative added, gouache, and mixed media, with a found metal binding.

0823 **Not to have, but to be** (6 x 14 x 2¼ in [15.2 x 35.6 x 5.7 cm]): Sculptural work with a paper vessel made of Spanish flax, box construction with book board and cloth, and two letterpress printed meditations in text and image on Kaji paper.

0824 **Ad Infinitum** (11¼ x 7¾ x ¾ in [28.1 x 19.4 x 1.9 cm]): Watercolor paper and thread.

0825 **Fashion Statement** (US size 6 [European size 36]): Wearable book made from quotes about fashion from Goethe, Mark Twain, Karl Lagerfeld, Sophia Loren, Chamfort, and Oscar Wilde. The text is cut and sewn from Tyvek. Dress designed by Elizabeth DeSole.

0826, 0827 **A Dog's Tale** (5 x 26 x 17 in [12.5 x 65.0 x 42.5 cm]): Sewn tulle pages with Print Gocco illustrations and inkjet printed text on Rives Lightweight on a silk pillow. The image gradually comes into focus and the story slowly shifts as the pages are turned.

0828, 0829, 0830 **Templum Elementorum** (22 in diameter [55.9 cm diameter]): A book sculpture with codices, co-authored with Taz Sibley. Sandblasted and painted glass cylinders containing books of metal, paper, and paper board with wire edge binding, all housed in a stenciled wood box.

0831 **Journey Jars #004 - 008** (4½ x 3 x 2½ in [11.3 x 7.5 x 6.3 cm]): Handmade paper, pastel, and natural materials. Left to right: #004 Basalt, Colorado; #005 565 Porch and Diane's Yard; #006 Amsten Beach, Ormond Beach, Florida; #007 Bailey's Mistake, Lubec, Maine; #008 New York Botanical Gardens, Bronx, New York.

0832, 0833 **Lovers Game** (3 x 13 x 10 in [7.5 x 32.5 x 25.0 cm]): Archival inkjet prints on Hahnemühle Copperplate paper, vintage metal watch parts cabinet with original glass vials.

0834, 0835 **Old-Fashioned Girl** (7 x 5 x 1¼ in [17.5 x 12.5 x 3.1 cm]): Vintage book by Louisa May Alcott, with an original collage poem and assemblage of found objects including glass tube with cork, feather, and burnt match.

0836 **In the Shadow** (6 x 12 x 6 in [15.0 x 30.0 x 15.0 cm]): Archival inkjet printing on silk organza of a digitally altered original photograph and text by Kobayashi Issa. Sewn with figure 8 bookbinding stitch and housed in acrylic.

0837 **Perpetual Calendar II** (3½ x 2 x 5 in [8.8 x 5.0 x 12.5 cm]): Spokes from an umbrella, handmade paper, beads, needles, and other mixed materials.

0838, 0839 **Waterfall** (6 x 4 x 4 in [15.0 x 10.0 x 10.0 cm]): Archival inkjet printing on silk organza of a digitally altered original photograph

and text by Yosa Buson. Sewn with figure 8 bookbinding stitch and housed in acrylic.

0840, 0841 **Amanuensis** (6 x 8 x 7¼ in [15.0 x 20.0 x 18.1 cm]): Twenty-four carat gold and Dobbin Mill papers on glass with original archival inkjet-printed text, and silk book cloth. Sculpture questions the signature as identity.

0842, 0843, 0844 **Niño Fidencio** (22 x 12 x 4 in [55.0 x 30.0 x 10.0 cm]): Original calligraphy and paintings in an accordion-fold book with Tyvek and dowel hinges housed in a wooden shrine festooned with holiday ornaments and found objects. The accordion holds a small codex that is the life story of this folk saint from Mexico, told in inkjet photos and original calligraphy.

0845 **Mama's Kitchen** (10 x 8 x 8 in [25.0 x 20.0 x 20.0 cm]): Wearable book of vintage wallpaper and fabric, with original text and illustrations in graphite and acrylic paint.

0846 **BookOpolis Crown** (14 x 14 x 13 in [35.0 x 35.0 x 32.5 cm]): Wearable book made from decorative paper, book pages, and fabric with graphite text.

0847, 0848 **Ryoanji** (9 x 6 x 4 in [22.5 x 15.0 x 10.0 cm]): Carved Japanese dictionary.

0849 **Pétra** (11½ x 8½ x 13 in [28.8 x 21.3 x 32.5 cm]): Carved Encyclopedia Britannica set, with added pigments.

0850 **Longmen** (13 x 22 x 9½ in [32.5 x 55.0 x 23.8 cm]): Eroded encyclopedias with mahogany.

0851, 0852 **Beginning** (12 x 4 x 3 in [30.0 x 10.0 x 7.5 cm]): Blown eggs containing original letterpress-printed text and related materials.

0853, 0854 **Toaster Book** (3 x 3 x 1½ in [7.5 x 7.5 x 3.8 cm]): Two accordion-fold books containing toast recipes that pop up via a hidden ribbon mechanism when the toaster-like case is opened.

0855 **Butter Butt** (3 x 7 x 3 in [7.5 x 17.5 x 7.5 cm]): Text transferred onto "butter pats" created with Cecile Webster's handmade pigmented cotton paper, connected with ribbons into a Jacob's Ladder structure. Cast cotton paper butter dish.

0856, 0857 **Tenure Grind** (8 x 15 x 1½ in [20.0 x 37.5 x 3.8 cm]): Text from the artist's promotion and tenure application printed on colored papers, hand-cut and curled, in a styrofoam meat pack, with shrink wrap and digitally-printed stickers.

0858, 0859 **Border Crossing: In the War Room** (19 x 22½ x ½ in [47.5 x 56.3 x 1.3 cm]): Cut atlas pages with zippers stitched onto the cut edges. Folios can be unfastened and refastened in a number of combinations, challenging the notions of geographical borders, and pages can be added or subtracted.

0860, 0861 **Vest of Knowledge** (63 x 35 x 20 in [157.5 x 87.5 x 50.0 cm]): Sixty-four altered volumes of the Encyclopedia Britannica as a loaded but undetonated "World Book," a weapon of knowledge and awe rather than shock and terror.

0862 **Mask** (12 x 7 x 7 in [30.0 x 17.5 x 17.5 cm]): Altered English dictionary, cut away in the shape of an ellipse. Portions of the text block and spine are removed to make the piece flexible, referencing "twisted" or "masked" words.

0863 **City** (16 x 16 x 36 in [40.0 x 40.0 x 90.0 cm]): Altered books created between 1990–1996 on a wood shelf. Original hardbound publications were mainly novels, plus philosophy books, a veterinary text, and and English-to-German dictionary, as a metaphor for the cross section of life, culture, and ideas common to a large municipality.

0864 **Vessels** (12 x 12 x 2½ in [30.0 30.0 x 6.3 cm]): Acrylic sheets and linen threads, single sheet coptic binding.

0865, 0866 **Ivanhoe** (20 x 12 x 4 in [50 x 30 x 10 cm]): Walter Scott's *Ivanhoe,* re-bound in binders board, leather, and original fragments from the first binding. With gold tooling.

0867 **Awakening** (43 x 6½ x 8 in [107.5 x 16.3 x 20.0 cm]): Engraved acrylic sheets and linen thread, single sheet coptic binding.

0868 **Relative Memory** (3¼ x 2¾ x 2¾ in [8.1 x 6.9 x 6.9 cm]): Adhesive bound glass pages with laser-printed Gampi and book cloth. Image revealed only on page edges.

0869, 0870 **Meditation** (10 x 8¼ x 8¼ in [25.0 20.6 x 20.6 cm]): Rusted paper with wire housed in an acrylic box.

0871 **Dreams** (9 x 3½ x 1½ in [22.5 x 8.8 x 3.8 cm]): Carved wood body covered with artist's handmade abaca/sewing patter paper, dyed with a black wash and accented with coins, nails, and fossil pieces. Book is coptic bound artist's handmade paper dyed with black wash, with altered personal photographs, various proverbs and quotes, and paper beads.

0872, 0873 **Complete Arithmetic** (13 x 4½ x 2½ in [32.5 x 11.3 x 6.3 cm]): Found vintage mathematics book and archival digital prints and mixed media including encaustic wax, housed in a vintage wooden box.

0874, 0875, 0876 **Spelling Bee** (12 x 3 x 3 in [30.0 x 7.5 x 7.5 cm]): Tintypes, archival digital prints, and other mixed media housed in a wooden box.

0877, 0878 **Temporary Shelters** (4 x 4½ x 4 in [10.0 x 11.3 x 10.0 cm]): Land snail shell housing a digital print of original typewritten text, packaged with dirt and a seed.

0879, 0880 **Sacred Poem, LXX, Sacred Poem LXIX, Sacred Poem LXVI**: Three works from the *Sacred Poem Series,* utilizing pages from the 1849 edition of *Parish Psalmody, A Collection of Psalms and Hynms for Public Worship* by Dr. Issac Watts, incorporating gold leaf, linen thread, and gampi tissue.

0881 **in movimento (moving)** (5 x 18 x 4 in [12.5 x 45.0 x 10.0 cm]): Altered and hand-bound book with stencil printing and experimental inks and moveable type.

0882 **Sacred Poem XLV** (7½ x 4 x 1¼ in [18.8 x 10.0 x 3.1 cm]): One piece from the *Sacred Poem Series,* utilizing pages from the 1844 edition of *Parish Psalmody, A Collection of Psalms and Hynms for Public Worship* by Dr. Issac Watts, cut and sewn, and incorporating gold leaf.

0883 **Exploring Australia** (9 x 12 x 12 in [22.5 x 30.0 x 30.0 cm]): *Exploring Australia* by Eve Pownall altered to fit over wooden kangaroo puzzle, with pages also cut and pasted to create a eucalypt forest.

0884, 0885 **SavedBooks58Humanity** (7½ x 13 x 7 in [18.8 x 32.5 x 17.5 cm]): Painted and distressed recycled book, hand-sewn pages.

0886, 0887 **Above the Eye** (6½ x 3¼ x 3¼ in [16.3 x 8.1 x 8.1 cm]): Circa 1880 hinged oak sewing attachment box with cast paper and artist's handmade papers of abaca, torch ginger grass, and black cotton rag gradated in the vat.

0888, 0889 **Fig Book** (7 x 11 x 3 in [17.5 x 27.5 x 7.5 cm]): Original, digitally printed coptic bound book housed in a papier-mâché sculpture made from handmade recycled banana and fig bast paper, and fig timber.

0890, 0891 **This Too Shall Pass** (7 x 13 x 4 in [17.5 x 32.5 x 10.0 cm]): Original illustrations and text by the artist and Henry David Thoreau, handwritten on self-made kozo, gampi, and demin paper with encaustic monotype prints. Various found natural objects. Inspired by Thoreau: "...find your eternity in each moment."

0892 **Mollusk** (6½ x 6 x 2¼ in [16.3 x 15.0 x 5.6 cm]): Folded tea-stained paper ovals and folded pinked vellum ovals, with a tapered headband ending in a single pearl.

0893, 0894 **Library of Alexandria** (5 x 7½ x 2 in [12.5 x 18.8 x 5.0 cm]): Altered book. Rolled and burned pages, wax, shellac, ink, and stamped.

0895, 0896 **Homework; Groton Window** (4½ feet x 5½ feet [1.4 x 1.7 m]): Site-specific installation using recycled domestic materials including 35 mm film, tea bags, wooden coffee stirrers, masking tape, band-aids, sugar packets, shredded documents, price tags, holiday tinsel, and other found objects.

0897, 0898 **INDU: Commensalists and Hand Me Downs** (12 x 14 x 3½ in [30.0 x 35.0 x 8.8 cm]): Laser engraved, maple/red oak box with inlaid steel and stone that folds inside out to reveal two letterpress printed essays, four relief prints, two etchings with transfers, C-prints, and one large drawing (reproduced as an archival inkjet print) to present a virtual tour of an urban National Park.

0899, 0900 **To Find One Way**: Original incense-burnt calligraphy of the Chinese character "Tao"—which has various meanings, including path or way—each designed by a different stamp engraver or calligrapher on Japanese paper (Sekishu).

0901, 0902 **Fairy Tales** (8½ x 5 x 1½ in [21.3 x 12.5 x 3.8 cm]): Mixed-media altered book made of vintage book cover, original prints, collage, and assemblage of found objects.

0903, 0904 **Led into Gilt** (24 x 12 x 2 in [60.0 x 30.0 x 5.0 cm]): Unprepared goat skin cover, traditional book materials and tools presented in unfinished states and used in unintended manners.

0905, 0906 **What would the neighbors think** (6 x 10½ x 10½ in [15.0 x 26.3 x 26.3 cm]): Artist's family's version of "Don't Ask, Don't Tell." Accordion-fold structure of archival inkjet prints of vintage family photos; book cloth, Momigami paper, museum board, wooden core, and collected objects.

0907 **Travelog** (16 x 16 x 3 in [40.0 x 40.0 x 7.5 cm]): An impractical travel companion featuring two casebound books integrated into laptop structure with globe, maps, and compasses. Covers of leather and marbled paper.

0908 **Untitled** (9¼ x 7½ x 2¼ in [23.1 x 18.8 x 5.6 cm]): Cut paper sculpture.

0909 **Storytellers** (24 x 12 x 3 in [60.0 x 30.0 x 7.5 cm]): Original text handwritten on Eames "Architecture" paper by Neenah, with covers of polyurethaned cardboard. Coptic binding. Handmade fabric statues.

0910, 0911 **her side of the story** (3 x 3 x 3 in [7.5 x 7.5 x 7.5 cm]): Thirty-six hand-painted wooden blocks with original haikus, allowing the audience to build their own story sequence.

0912, 0913 **Sin Weavers** (2¾ x 7 x 3½ in [6.9 x 17.5 x 8.8 cm]): Bookboard box covered with handmade Cave paper with a natural walnut pigment and wax stains. Inside cover and lining paper is a gelatin print with sepia ink handwriting. Interior of woven-color cotton cords on a dowel representing Khipu (talking knots), the recording language of the Inca.

0914 **Homage to Hannelore** (5 x 5½ x 1 in [12.5 x 13.8 x 2.5 cm]): Altered book with a quote from the collage artist Hannelore Baron: an original assemblage incorporating fabric, rubber, and metal.

0915 **Licorice Allsorts** (8 x 4 x 1¼ in [20.0 x 10.0 x 3.1 cm]): Small book structures of guillotined paper bound with flexible industrial PVA and sealed in a commercial candy bag.

0916 **Thumbelina** (1 x 1⅓ x ¾ in [2.5 x 3.3 x 1.9 cm]): Hans Christian Andersen's *Thumbelina* in a minature shaped binding enclosed in gilded walnut shell. Computer-generated printing on handmade paper.

0917 **Hands of Josephus, Part II** (10½ x 4 x 37 in [26.3 x 10.0 x 92.5 cm]): Altered book (*Josephus: History of the Jews*), cut into hand shapes and sewn with Czech glass beads, with glove dryers as cover boards. The hand of the victor seems to control every version of the truth.

0918 **Batter My Heart: A Wall Street Valentine** (10 x 9 x 7 in [25.0 x 22.5 x 17.5 cm]): John Donne's poem of questioning faith, in a small accordion book with digital printing and Xerox transfers encased in an acrylic-painted girdle stuck with pins, and holding shredded money.

0919 **Unborn Thoughts** (4 x 5 x 4 in [10.0 x 12.5 x 10.0 cm]): Collection of scroll books with original handwritten text on parchment paper, housed in chestnut shells with cotton batting in a paper vessel with hand-stitching. Celebrating of life and the beauty contained within.

0920, 0921 **The Banalities of Motherhood** (2 x 12 x 11 in [5.0 x 30.0 x 27.5 cm]): Silk screened original text from grocery lists on cotton paper dyed with commercial dyes and Tang, punched and strung into a wearable book inspired by sixteenth-century Flemish neckware.

0922 **Talking in Circles** (6 x 8 x 7 in [15 x 20.0 x 17.5 cm]): Inkjet printed text on Japanese mulberry paper, pamphlet stitched and accented with waxed linen thread, acrylic, and antique buttons.

0923, 0924 **Still Sense** (2¾ x 2¾ x 2¾ in [6.9 x 6.9 x 6.9 cm]): Three hinged relief boxes with loose pages in slipcases, original text and illustrations printed with intaglio and screen printing, with added specimens and mixed media.

0925 **Pocket Guides** (9⅛ x 6¼ x ⅜ in [22.8 x 15.6 x 0.9 cm]): Three volumes made from a mold of a single book and cast in different grades of rubber, with two of the three volumes embedded with paper pages.

0926 **Book of Sculptures** (5¾ x 4 x 1¾ in [14.4 x 10.0 x 4.4 cm]): Unique artist book made with white marble and metal letters.

0927, 0928 **That's Life** (30 x 35 x 12 in [75.0 x 87.5 x 30.0 cm]): Cover of cast and hand-shaped kozo fiber, tinted with walnut dye and stain, and with oak inserts. Interior of handmade hand-shaped abaca, abaca/flax, and flax papers, and hand-painted dyes.

0929 **Recapitulation** (10 x 72 x 10¼ in [25.0 x 180.0 x 25.6 cm]): Sculptural book installation made from pulped discarded book blocks.

0930, 0931 **A Primer for Democracy** (3 x 3 x 3 in [7.5 x 7.5 x 7.5 cm]): Letterpress printed in two colors from hand-set type, die-cut to create interlocking pieces. Orignal text that expresses elements that create and sustain democracy, by the artist with class participants Dawn Endean, Patricia Halsell, Kaylea Trowbridge, and Elizabeth Walters.

0932 **BookEnviron: Twin Path** (8½ x 20 x 14 feet [2.6 x 6.1 x 4.3 m]): Handmade paper of abaca fibers, threads, tea, hair, and branches hung by embedded threads defining two spiraling pathways, which intertwine and envelop viewers.

0933, 0934 **Vishnu Crew Stews Vindaloo Anew** (9½ in diameter [23.8 cm diameter]): Four accordion books bolted to hinged aluminum volvelle, housed in a film can lined with industrial felt. Original linocut illustration, hand-set metal type letterpress printed on Khadi Indian handmade paper.

0935 **Document Storage V** (7¾ x 5 x 5½ in [19.4 x 12.5 x 13.8 cm]): A small concertina book, housed in a box with an embracing 2nd box and a 3rd box enclosing both, with all box surfaces covered by intaglio prints and brush and ink drawings on Japanese paper.

0936 **Collected Stories** (21 x 9 x 2 in [52.5 x 22.5 x 5.0 cm]): Original calligraphy and acrylic paint with found text and painted paper and cardboard.

0937, 0938, 0939 **Hole in My Heart** (⅝ x 13 x 13 in [1.6 x 32.5 x 32.5 cm]): Intaglio prints on Japanese paper cover hinged foam core blocks, four hiding letterpress booklets of translations of Japanese women's poems of the ninth to thirteenth centuries.

0940, 0941 **Babylon/Babble-on** (96 x 126 x 24 in [240 x 315 x 60 cm]): Sculptural installation with handwritten and illuminated original short story and photographs. Book constructed of sheet metal and wooden binding with leather hinge, lead-covered nails, photographs, and pastels, with letterpress printed text on rag paper. Sculpture constructed of sheet metal, plywood, cardboard, Plexiglass, and acrylic paint on stretched canvas.

0942, 0943 **Behind Anderson's Camera** (8½ x 8½ x 3¼ in [21.3 x 21.3 x 8.1 cm]): Dimensionally accurate representation of J. Fred Anderson's camera made from camera leather, lacquered wood, hinges, and photographs. Includes computer-generated text, and copies of Anderson's photographs.

0944, 0945 **caught (cause, calm, and chaos)** (6¾ x 6 x ¼ in [16.9 x 15.0 x 0.6 cm]): Visual poem of three hand-stitched codexes, to be folded together as a sculpture; are made from a variety of accumulated papers and out-takes, old and new images, acrylic paint, gouache, and ink.

0946 **Forgotten Knowledge** (33 x 36 x 9 in [82.5 x 90.0 x 22.5 cm]): Found objects contained within an altered 25 volume Funk & Wagnall's Encylopedia set.

0947 **Shield Book: Relic of Resolve** (9½ x 7 x 2½ in [23.8 x 17.5 x 6.3 cm]): Assemblage of found and altered book with folded pages, sewing, embroidery, and collage utilizing feathers, moss, papier-mâché, and other mixed media.

0948, 0949 **Yet** (8 x 12 x 4 in [20.0 x 30.0 x 10.0 cm]): Original photogravure printed with a polymer plate on Hahnemühle etching paper, book about hope and despair bound from bark papers, interior of digitally-printed text on Niyodo natural paper, cradled in an antique mirrored box.

0950, 0951, 0952 **Mountain Tops** (14 x 11 x 11 in [35.0 x 27.5 x 27.5 cm]): Watercut aluminum from original poetry, prints, and drawings, with C-prints mounted on aluminum presented in a canvas sling with teak handles is an homage to a mentor, and a community.

0953 **My Life is an Open Book** (24 x 9½ x 2½ in [60.0 x 23.8 x 6.3 cm]): Dried California lotus stalks and wire pages, painted dowels for spine, beads and thread accents.

0954 **Pages from a Landscape** (3¼ x 14 x 3¾ in [8.1 x 35.0 x 9.4 cm]): Pamphlet-bound leaf papers, kozo paper, and plant-fiber papers housed in found bark.

0955, 0956 **(S)Edition** (19 x 15 x 16-18 in [47.5 x 37.5 x 40.0-45.0 cm]): Cast and hand-shaped dyed handmade abaca paper embellished with cotton rag. Edition of 99 copies, and an installation that imagines books proliferating like fungi, surreptitiously initiating change.

0957 Textual Armament (14 x 12 x 7 in [35.0 x 30.0 x 17.5 cm]): Sculptural book of encaustic wax-dipped found paper wrapped in black denim handmade paper encircling handmade gelatin/mica-coated handmade Abaca paper.

0958 Heart of No Peace: Our War in Afghanistan (2½ x 2½ x 29¾ in [6.3 x 6.3 x 74.4 cm]): Handwritten and hand-stamped text on paper, embroidery thread binding with needle still attached, and additional blank pages.

0959, 0960, 0961 Dixie Compass Sculptural Book (24 x 24 x 6 in [60 x 60 x 15 cm]): Three original short stories letterpress printed with wooden type, linotype, hand-set type, and photopolymer plates. Original woodcuts and silver print photos with letterpress impressions.

0962, 0963, 0964 Ocean Wave (15 x 14½ x 2 in [37.5 x 36.3 x 5.0 cm]): Multi-panel cut paper 3D sculpture in hardbound case, with multi-color reduction linocut print. Extends from 2 to 45 inches (5.0 to 112.5 cm).

0965, 0966 Unfolding Each Day (6 x 6 x 6 in [15.0 x 15.0 x 15.0 cm]): A year's personal journal, remembered with inkjet printing of original artwork in a box with metal rods and magnets.

0967 Tea Book (5 x 5 x 1¾ in [12.5 x 12.5 x 4.4 cm]): Tea bags, rope, and stained wood.

0968, 0969 The Village Type (17 x 32 x 1½ in [42.5 x 80.0 x 3.8 cm]): Anecdotes about each letter in a California job case are printed on canvas that folds, like the cover of a book, over the case filled with folded paper.

0970 Tribus Equus (8 x 8 x 5 in [20.0 x 20.0 x 12.5 cm]): Torn slabs of Raku clay pages, bisque fired then drawn on with wax resist technique. Glazed and raku fired with wood chip reduction, and bound with horse hair.

0971 Unnatural Histories No. 33: Seaside Stories (6¾ x 7¾ x 3 in [16.9 x 19.4 x 7.5 cm]): Digitally printed Moab Entrada Rag paper with original text and illustrations, both covering and folded into a cigar box.

0972 Siren/Vampire Glass Book (26 x 18 x 13 in [65.0 x 45.0 x 32.5 cm]): Original silk screen with sand blasting and enamel painting on glass, with a metal stand by Robert Roesch.

0973 A Simple History of the Atmosphere (10 x 14½ x 2½ in [25.0 x 36.3 x 6.3 cm]): Explores life-threatening shifts in environmental balance. Original artwork in relief and mono printing and letterpress printed text on Hahnemühle Ingres paper; box construction with book cloth.

0974, 0975 Famopily (18¾ x 18¾ x ¼ in [46.9 x 46.9 x 0.6 cm]): Original text and illustrations inkjet printed on paper with book cloth and binder's board.

0976 Tora Bora: An Opera in Three Acts (12⅛ x 13⅛ x 1¼ in [30.3 x 32.8 x 3.1 cm]): Fold-out stage with multiple backdrops and a letterpress printed booklet designed by Klaus-Ulrich Rötzscher. Original illustrations and text, screen prints of puppets and stage backdrops, and six copper engravings.

0977 Stacking Ormond Beach (4 x 2 x 5 in (total, stack of three) [10.0 x 5.0 x 12.5 cm]): Handmade paper, natural materials, and pastel.

0978, 0979 Admonition or Meditation #1 (10 x 6½ x ½ in [25.0 x 16.3 x 1.3 cm]): English and shorthand words formed with felt and wire, then stitched onto wire frames.

0980 Elusive (10 x 7½ x 10 in [25.0 x 18.8 x 25.0 cm]): Artist's wood-fired clay castings from original rubber relief molds with added incised

original text about human placement: Earth, time, and space. Accordion binding with waxed linen thread.

0981 The Right to Contradiction (7 x 5½ x 1⅓ in [17.5 x 13.8 x 3.3 cm]): Handmade box set with poems by Stergios Chatzikyriakidis and illustrations by Lina Avramidou, inkjet-printed and sewn into brown paper bags which must be torn open to be read.

0982 The Root (27¾ x 17 x ¼ in [70.5 x 43.2 x .6 cm]): Made of book-board, Italian printed paper and book cloth. Methods include a typewriter, lino-cut prints, and Prisma markers.

0984, 0985 The Night Hunter (12 x 9¼ x 2½ in [30.0 x 23.1 x 6.3 cm]): Palm leaf book with poem by Nancy Campbell, text printed from hand-set type and original illustrations from polymer plates. Includes a carved wooden game board with rawhide pouch containing sculptural pieces of metal, soapstone ,and a bone.

0986, 0987 Reliquary (13½ x 5¼ x 3 in [33.8 x 13.1 x 7.5 cm]): Three codex books, *Metacarpals, Nexus,* and *Relics;* and twelve twigs housed in a handmade box. Books contain sepia pencil renderings on handmade abaca and cotton paper; box and covers are made from handmade flax paper and book board.

0988, 0989, 0990 Lizard Box: If you try to capture magic it dies or disappears (5½ x 4⅜ x 4¼ in [13.8 x 10.9 x 10.6 cm]): Clamshell box with drawers containing shells, mica, lizard, replica of a pre-Columbian Mayan sculpture, also housing an accordion-fold book with original SX70 photos and handwritten text.

0991, 0992 The Curious Journey (3 x 3 x 1 in [7.5 x 7.5 x 2.5 cm]): Relief carved print on papers from Nepal, Tibet, and Thailand, with an enclosed coptic bound miniature book.

0993 Too Much Order (6½ x 8¾ x 1 in [16.3 x 21.9 x 2.5 cm]): A fable about fear inhibiting one's actions. Pop-up book with original text made with Lama Li paper and digital paper.

0994, 0995 Sheets (6 x 4½ x 2½ in [15.0 x 11.3 x 6.3 cm]): Four seasonal homeless haiku by Dolores Connelly letterpress printed with hand-set metal type on handmade abaca paper.

0996, 0997 Religio Mathmatica (9 x 9½ x 9½ in [22.5 x 23.8 x 23.8 cm]): Sculptural book of spattered paste paper on paper board. Wire edge binding. Housed in a yew wood box.

0998 Collection (10 x 5 x 5 in [25.0 x 12.5 x 12.5 cm]): Three books with Ethiopian and Coptic bindings, with wood scraps from Stony Lamar, Jim Croft, and Frank Wiesner, and mica, fossils, bones, shells, stones, and handmade paper.

0999, 1000 The First Amendment: Reliquary for the Ashes of Salman Rushdie's Satanic Verses (12 x 12 x 12 in [30.0 x 30.0 x 30.0 cm]): Sealed reliquary made from inkjet on paper laminated to binder's board with polyurethane and UV filter coatings, stained glass, and gold leaf. Felt-covered wood base with gold stamped text of the *The First Amendment* of the United States. Burnt copy of Salman Rushdie's *Satanic Verses* housed inside reliquary.

Directory of Artists

Miyako Akai, Kototsubo, JAPAN
am@miobox.jp
http://kototsubo.com
0139, 0140, 0197, 0198, 0679, 0680

Jody Alexander, USA
jojalex@comcast.net
www.jalexbooks.com
0697–0703

**Michael Andrews,
Bombshelter Press**, USA
michael@mdaarts.com
www.mdaarts.com
0150, 0151

Sharon Armstead, AUSTRALIA
armsha@tpg.com.au
0954

**Alice Armstrong,
Flotsam Studio**, USA
aarmstrong9@yahoo.com
0587, 0588

Eileen Arnow-Levine, USA
arnowart@verizon.net
www.arnowart.com
0135, 0136

Rachael Ashe, CANADA
rkashe@gmail.com
http://rachaelashe.com
0946

Alice Austin, Artist Books, USA
alice@amaustin.com
www.amaustin.com
0381, 0382, 0423, 0424

**Lisa Avramidou,
Schema Books**, UK
schemabooks@gmail.com
www.schemabooks.blogspot.com
0981

Alicia Bailey, USA
aliciabailey@mac.com
www.aliciabailey.com
0166–0168

Ruth Bardenstein, USA
ruthbpc@sbcglobal.net
0431

Suzanne Barnes, USA
suzanne.barnes@massart.edu
0986, 0987

Libby Barrett, USA
adlibartstudio@gmail.com
www.libbybarrett.net
0731

Julie Baugnet, USA
jabaugnet@stcloudstate.edu
www.juliebaugnet.blogspot.com/
0243, 0244

Lucy Baxandall, UK
lucybax@yahoo.com
www.lucybaxandall.com
0146, 0147

**Margaret Beech,
Calligrapher & Bookartist**, UK
margaret@beeches13.freeserve.
co.uk
http://beeches13.skyrock.com
0130

Jeanne Bennett, USA
fepper@windstream.net
098

Jill K. Berry, USA
jill@jillberrydesign.com
www.jillberrydesign.com
0152–0154, 0666, 0667, 0842–0844

Doug Beube, USA
dbeube@mindspring.com
www.dougbeube.com
0858–0863

Andrew Binder, USA
abinder6@me.com
http://www.coe.fau.edu/faculty/
abinder
0185, 0186

Jerry Bleem, USA
bleemjerry@aol.com
www.jerrybleem.com
0179, 0180, 0474

**Sarah Bodman,
Bookarts at the Centre
for Fine Print Research**, UK
Sarah.Bodman@uwe.ac.uk
www.bookarts.uwe.ac.uk
0406, 0407, 0803

**Velma Bolyard,
Wake Robin Papers**, USA
vdbolyard@gmail.com
www.velmabolyard.blogspot.com
0084, 0085

e Bond, roughdrAft books, USA
roughdrAftbooks@gmail.com
www.roughdraftbooks.com
0046, 0910, 0911

Mary Beth Boone, USA
mboone4102@att.net
www.marybethboone.com
0491, 0492

Jim Bové, USA
jimbove@hotmail.com
http://crafthaus.ning.com
0183, 0184

Barbara Brear, BB Miniatures,
SOUTH AFRICA
bbminiatures@yahoo.com
www.bbminiatures.homestead.
com
0193–0196

**Tara Bryan,
walking bird press**, CANADA
tarabryan@gmail.com
www.tarabryan.com
0425–0427

Dave Buchen, PUERTO RICO
davebuchen@yahoo.com
www.davebuchen.wordpress.com
0307, 0308

**Lark Burkhart,
Jumping Crow Studio**, USA
larkhere@cox.net
www.jumpingcrowstudio.com
0953, 0958

**Ginger Burrell,
Midnight Moon Press**, USA
ginger@rkg.com
www.gingerburrell.com
0487, 0525

Warren K. Buss, Naos Press, USA
info@naospress.com
www.naospress.com
0535, 0536

Barbara Bussolari, USA
bussolari1@frontier.com
www.barbarabussolari.com
0400, 0401, 0454, 0455, 0871

Kay Byrne, IRELAND
imajica@eircom.net
0473

**Elissa R. Campbell,
Blue Roof Designs**, USA
elissaA@blueroofdesigns.com
www.blueroofdesigns.com
0443

Elizabeth Carls, USA
elizabeth.c.carls@gmail.com
www.elizabethcarls.com
0245, 0246

Antonio Claudio Carvalho, BRAZIL
artrat@uol.com.br
0926

**Rebecca Chamlee,
Pie In The Sky Press**, USA
pieintheskypress@mac.com
www.pieintheskypress.com; www.
pieintheskypress@blogspot.com
0176, 0177

MalPina Chan, USA
malpina@yahoo.com
www.malpinachan.com
0374, 0375, 0539

Julie Chen, Flying Fish Press, USA
jchen@flyingfishpress.com
www.flyingfishpress.com
0070–0073, 0475–0477

**Julie Chen and
Clifton Meador**, USA
clifton.meador@gmail.com
www.cliftonmeador.com
0479–0481

**Lisa Cheney-Jorgensen,
RightSide Design**, USA
lcjorge@cableone.net
www.lisacheneyjorgensen@
blogspot.com
0161, 0162

Elaine G. Chu, USA
egc@egchu.com
www.egchu.com
0626, 0627

**Rachelle W. Chuang, Rachelle W.
Chuang Art & Design**, USA
rachellewchuangA@gmail.com
www.rachellewchuang.com
0396–0398, 0957

Margaret Couch Cogswell, USA
mccogswell@charter.net
www.margaretcouchcogswell.com
0728–0730, 0845, 0846

Matt Cohen, C & C Press, USA
matt@candcpress.com
www.candcpress.com
0642, 0643

Cynthia Colbert, USA
colbertc@mailbox.sc.edu
0009, 0010, 0328, 0338

Sas Colby, USA
sas@sascolby.com
www.sascolby.com
0039–0041, 0124, 0125

Susan Collard, USA
smcollard@gmail.com
www.susancollard.com
0722–0726

Dee Collins, USA
deecollinsart@gmail.com
www.deecollins.com
0047, 0048

Béatrice Coron, USA
webmail@beatricecoron.com
www.beatricecoron.com
0404, 0405, 0706, 0825

Laurie Corral, BookWorks, USA
laurie@ashevillebookworks.com
www.ashevillebookworks.com
0709–0714

Guylaine Couture, CANADA
gycouture@gmail.com
www.gycouture.com
0128, 0129, 0668, 0669

**Jenny Craig,
Notta Pixie Press**, USA
jennybeast@mindspring.com
www.nottapixiepress.etsy.com
0511, 0512

Melissa Jay Craig, USA
melissajaycraig@mac.com
http://web.me.com/melissajaycraig
0141–0143, 0927, 0928, 0955, 0956

Katherine D. Crone, USA
kcrone@nyc.rr.com
www.katherinedcrone.com
0776, 0836, 0838, 0839

Heather Crossley, AUSTRALIA
mkhc@powerup.com.au
http://homepage.powerup.com.
au/~mkhc
0120, 0837

Eleonora Cumer, ITALY
info@eleonoracumer.com
www.eleonoracumer.com
0447, 0448, 0638, 0639, 0881

**Kerri Cushman,
performing goats press**, USA
cushwoman@hotmailcom
www.kerricushman.com
0652, 0653, 0790, 0791, 0855

Amanda D'Amico, USA
tiny.revoutionary@gmail.com
www.tinyrevolutionarypress.com
0526, 0527

Robyn A. Daniel, USA
robyndaniel@verizon.net
0380, 0978, 0979

**Steven C. Dauber,
Red Trillium Press**, USA
steve@redtrilliumpress.com
www.redtrilliumpress.com
0352, 0353, 0688

Betsy Davids, USA
betsydavids@earthlink.net
0181, 0182, 0767–0769

Bryson Dean-Gauthier, USA
brysondean@comcast.net
http://mbrysondean.blogspot.com
0309, 0310

**Cathy DeForest,
Jubilation Press**, USA
cathy@jubilationpress.com
www.jubilationpress.com
0496, 0948, 0949

**Kirstin Demer,
Green Trike Press**, USA
greentrikepress@gmail.com
www.greentrikepress.com; www.
kirstindemer.com
0217, 0218, 0550, 0551

Brian Dettmer, USA
info@briandettmer.com
www.briandettmer.com
0795–0799, 0804, 0805

Susan Mackin Dolan, USA
sumac@comcast.net
http://artistsregister.com/artists/
co248
0416

**Sandra T. Donabed,
Ganymede Studio**, USA
sdonabed@mac.com
www.sandydonabed.com
0644, 0645, 0785, 0786

Dayle Doroshow, Zingaro, USA
dayledoroshow@hotmail.com
www.dayledoroshow.com
0163, 0513, 0514

Carly Drew, USA
carly.d.drew@gmail.com
www.carly-drew.com
www.carlydrew.carbonmade.com
0543

Tracie Morris Easler, USA
tracieeasler@yahoo.com
www.tracieeasler.com
0970

Dorit Elisha, USA
dorit_elisha@yahoo.com
www.doritelisha.com
0901, 0902

Elsi Vassdal Ellis, EVE Press, USA
eve_press@yahoo.com
0112–0114, 0117–119, 0121–0123

Timothy C. Ely, USA
t.ely@mac.com
www.timothyely.com
0076, 0077, 0236–0238, 0252–0254

Arlyn Ende, USA
arlyn.ende@gmail.com
http://sites.google.com/site/arly-
nende
0449, 0450

Daniel Essig, USA
books@danielessig.com
www.danielessig,com
0001–0004, 0727, 0998

Isabelle Faivre, FRANCE
faivreberthier@free.fr
http://meslivresinsolites.blogspot.
com
0509, 0510, 0908

**Lauren Faulkenberry,
Firebrand Press**, USA
insculpo@hotmail.com
www.firebrandpress.org
0517, 0540–0542

Sandra C. Fernandez, USA
studio@sandrafernandez.info
www.sandrafernandez.info
0765, 0766

Cari Ferraro, USA
cariscribe@gmail.com
www.cariferraro.com
0544, 0545

Dorothy Field, CANADA
dotter@seaside.net
0655, 0657, 0658

Dea Fischer, rock-paper-scissors,
CANADA
rock-paper-scissors@live.ca
www.thestarbook.wordpress.com
0408, 0409

**Nancy A. Fiumera,
The Studio at Far Enough**, USA
far-enough@att.net
www.far-enough.com
0189–0192

**Foolscap Press, Lawrence G.
Van Veleer, Peggy Gotthold**, USA
foolscap@cruzio.com
www.foolscappress.com
0484, 0719–0721

Ke Francis, Hoopsnake Press, USA
madisonfrancis@bellsouth.net
www.hoopsnakepress.com
0940, 0941, 0959–0961

Mara Jevera Fulmer, USA
mara@lookinglassdesign.com
www.lookinglassdesign.com
0649–0651

Anne C. Gable, USA
gable.annec@gmail.com
http://acgable.typepad.com
0925

Jackie Gardener, USA
jackie@mcn.org
www.jackiegardener.com; www.
jackigardener.blogspot.com
0367–0369, 0538

Madelyn Garrett, USA
madega@comcast.net
www.studioissima.com
0199, 0321–0323, 0327

Susan Kapuscinski Gaylord, USA
susan@susangaylord.com
www.susangaylord.com
0144, 0145

Annette Geistfeld, USA
annettegeistfeld@mac.com
www.annettegeistfeld.com
0534

Jeanne Germani, CANADA
jgermani@sympatico.ca
www.jeannegermani.com
0171, 0172, 0531

**Pamela S. Gibson,
ThistlePaper Press**, USA
pamela@thistlepaper.net
0378

Anne Gilman, USA
gilmananne@gmail.com
www.anngilman.com
0689

Anià Gilmore, USA
design@aniaart.com
www.aniaartstudio.com
0893, 0894

**Ania Gilmore and Annie
Zeybekoglu**, USA
design@aniaart.com,
annniezey@gmail.com
www.aniaartstudio.com
www.anniezey.com
0781, 0782

Donna Globus, USA
donnaglobus@verizon.net
0968, 0969

**Alisa Golden,
never mind the press**, USA
www.neverbook.com
0005, 0006, 0133, 0134, 0265, 0266

Judith Golden, USA
judithgolden@earthlink.net
www.judithgolden.com
0988–0990

Mary Goldthwaite-Gagne, USA
marydgoldthwaite@gmail.com
www.marygoldthwaitegagne.com
0684

Ellen Gradman, USA
sparkyourart@me.com
www.sparkyourart.com
0291, 0292, 0770

**Patricia Grass,
Green Heron Book Arts**, USA
pagrass@aol.com
www.greenheronbookkits.com
0704, 0705

Anne G. Greenwood, USA
annegreenwood.net@gmail.com
www.annegreenwood.net
0210, 0211

Marvel Grégoire, USA
mgregoire@q.com
0209, 0537

Alicia Griswold, USA
agrisworld@me.com
www.sendingpagesouttodry@
blogspot.com
0518, 0519

Roni Gross, Z'roah Press, USA
rgd6@verizon.net
www.ronigross.com
0523, 0524, 0984, 0985

Suzanne S. Hall, USA
susi7@frontier.com
www.workswithpaper.com
0305, 0306

**Frank Hamrick,
Old Fan Press**, USA
fhamrick@me.com
www.frankhamrick.com
0204–0206

Karen Hanmer, USA
karen@karenhanmer.com
www.karenhanmer.com
0331, 0332, 0356–0358, 0694, 0974, 0975

Lisa Hasegawa, ilfant press, USA
lisa@ilfant.com
www.ilfant.com
0505, 0808–0810

**Meghan Hawkes,
Meghan Hawkes Photography
& Bookarts**, USA
meghanhawkes@gmail.com
info@meghanhawkes.com
www.meghanhawkes.com
0982, 0983

Susannah Hays, Venus Pencils, USA
sunprint@earthlink.net
www.susannahhays.com
0521, 0522

Art Hazelwood, USA
arthur@arthazelwood.com
www.arthazelwood.com
0515, 0516, 0976

Charlotte Hedlund, USA
ch4art@aol.com
www.charlottehedlund.com
0501, 0502, 0695, 0696

Caren Heft, Arcadian Press, USA
cheft@uwsp.edu
www.uwsp.edu/art-design/cheft/
arcadia
0034–0036

**Margery S. Hellmann,
The Holburne Press**, USA
mshellmann@comcast.net
0203

Lauren Henkin, Vela Noche, USA
lauren@laurenhenkin.com
www.laurenhenkin.com
0207, 0208

**Michael A. Henninger,
Rat Art Press**, USA
michael@ratartpress.com
www.ratartpress.com
0532, 0533

Paul Henry, UK
info@paulhenrydesign.com
www.paulhenrydesign.com
0007, 0008, 0016–0018, 0329, 0330

**Annie E. Herlocker,
Paper Revival Press**, USA
aeherlocker@gmail.com
0212

**Helen Hiebert,
Helen Hiebert Studio**, USA
helen@helenhiebertstudio.com
www.helenhiebertstudio.com
0758, 0759

Debbie Hill, AUSTRALIA
debhill04@yahoo.com.au
www.debbiehill.com.au
0348, 0349

Turner Hilliker, USA
turnerhilliker@gmail.com
www.turnerhilliker.com
0235

Jennifer Hines, USA
jennifer@jenniferhines.net
www.jenniferhines.net
0294–0296

Judith Hoffman, USA
art@judithhoffman.net
www.judithhoffman.net
0030, 0031, 0463, 0634–0636

Elizabeth Holster, USA
bholster@hotmail.com
www.holsterfinearts.blogspot.com
0520, 0604

Suzanne Reese Horvitz, USA
suzannehorvitz@comcast.net
www.suzannehorvitz.com
0676, 0742, 0972

**Robyn Hunt,
Robin Sparrow Books**,
NEW ZEALAND
robyn-hunt@xtra.co.nz
www.robinsparrowbooks@xtra.
co.nz
0037, 0038

Andrew Huot, Tank Dive Press,
USA
andrewhuot@gmail.com
www.andrewhuot.com
0229, 0230, 0556, 0675

**Thomas Ingmire,
Scriptorium St. Francis**, USA
thomas@thomasingmire.com
www.scriptsf.com; www.thomas-
ingmire.com
0187, 0188, 0232–0234

Kimberly Izenman, USA
kizenman@mindspring.com
http://kizenman.blogspot.com
0227, 0228

Diane Jacobs, Scantron Press, USA
dianejacobs@igc.org
www.dianejacobs.net
0672–0674, 0788, 0789

**Renee Jarmolowicz,
Artist Alcove**, USA
rjarmolowicz@
collegeforcreativestudies.edu
0445, 0446

Barbara Johnston, CANADA
bjbookartist@gmail.com
0560

**Peggy Johnston,
Waveland Studio**, USA
wavelandstudio@att.net
www.wavelandstudio.com
0346, 0347, 0892

Nina Judin, Nina Judin Books,
THE NETHERLANDS
ninajudinbooks@gmail.com
www.ninajudin.com
0692, 0693

Sun Young Kang, USA
kangsy77@gmail.com
www.sunyoungkang.com
0436, 0437, 0899, 0900

Richard Kegler, USA
richard@wnybookarts.org
0334, 0903, 0904, 0907

Lynne Kelly, USA
blynnekelly@msn.com
www.yourlifegoeshere.com
0853, 0854

**Daniel E. Kelm,
Wide Awake Garage**, USA
daniel.kelm@mac.com
www.danielkelm.com
0336, 0337, 0597, 0598, 0828–0830,
0996, 0997

Marie Kelzer, USA
info@mariekelzerdesigns.com
www.mariekelzerdesigns.com
0222, 0223

**Friedrich Kerksieck,
Small Fires Press**, USA
smallfirespress@yahoo.com
www.smallfirespress.com
0683

**Ellen Knudson,
Crooked Letter Press**, USA
ellen@crookedletterpress.com
www.crookedletterpress.com
0052, 0053, 0231

Deborah Kogan, USA
0101, 0102, 0419, 0420

Eunkang Koh, USA
eunkangkohart@gmail.com
www.eunkangkoh.net
0601–0603

Lisa Kokin, USA
lisa@lisakokin.com
www.lisakokin.com
0760, 0929

Kumi Korf, USA
kumi@exeisland.com
www.kumikorf.com
0935, 0937-0939

**Dorothy Simpson Krause,
Viewpoint Editions**, USA
dotkrause@dotkrause.com
www.DotKrause.com
0099, 0100, 0389–0391

**Karen Kunc,
Blue Heron Press**, USA
kkunc1@unl.edu
www.karen-kunc.com
0148, 0149, 0482, 0483, 0485, 0486

Carole P. Kunstadt, USA
ckunstadt@gmail.com
www.carolekunstadt.com
0879, 0880, 0882

**Hilke Kurzke, Büchertiger Studio
& Press**, GERMANY
contact@buechertiger.de
http://buechertiger.de
0299, 0919

Hedi Kyle, USA
hedikyle@comcast.net
0303, 0304, 0355, 0503, 0504, 0507,
0508

**Mary Laird,
Quelque fois Press**, USA
risalalaird@gmail.com
0377

Monique Lallier, USA
folium@triad.rr.com
www.moniquelallier.com
0333, 0339

Margaret Lammerts, CANADA
ed.marg@telus.net
0269, 0270

**Joseph Lappie,
Peptic Robots Press**, USA
pepticrobot@pepticrobotpress.com
www.pepticrobotpress.com
0247–0249

Guy Laramée, CANADA
guylaramee@cooptel.qc.ca
www.guylaramee.com
0847–0850

**Roberta Lavadour,
Mission Creek Press**, USA
robertalavadour@gmail.com
www.missioncreekpress.com
0213, 0214, 0399, 0868

Aimee Lee, USA
contact@aimeelee.net
www.aimeelee.net
0089, 0090, 0108, 0109

Sammy Lee, Studio SML/K, USA
sammy@studiosmlk.com
www.studiosmlk.com
0373, 0965, 0966

Mia Leijonstedt, UK
enquiries@leijonstedt.com
www.leijonstedt.com
0219–0221, 0640, 0641, 0732

**Sue Huggins Leopard,
Leopard Studio Editions**, USA
sueleopard@mac.com
0392, 0813, 0814

**Annie Fain Liden,
A. Fain Books**, USA
anniefain@afainbooks.com
www.afainbooks.com
0215, 0216

Marianne Little, AUSTRALIA
mflit@melbpc.org.au
0546, 0547

Annell Livingston, USA
annell@taosnet.com
www.annelllivingston.com
0774, 0775, 0777–0780

Elysia Lock, USA
elysialock@gmail.com
www.evildarkgirl.com
0178

Viviana Lombrozo, USA
viviana@san.rr.com
www.vivianalombrozo.net
0817, 0936

Ann Lovett, USA
www.annlovett.com
0489, 0490, 0493, 0494

Julie Shaw Lutts, USA
julieshawlutts@gmail.com
www.julieshawlutts.com
0872–0876

Joan Lyons, USA
joan@joanlyons.com
www.joanlyons.com
0173–0175

Peter Madden, USA
peter@petermadden.com
www.petermadden.com
0074, 0075, 0095–0097, 0646, 0895,
0896

Leslie M. Madigan, USA
madigan5652@gmail.com
www.lesliemadigan.com
0831, 0977

Marlis Maehrle, GERMANY
post@papierzeichen.de
www.papierzeichen.de
0570, 0571, 0735

**Susan Makov,
Green Cat Press**, USA
smakov@live.com
www.greencatpress,com
0466, 0467

Helen Malone, AUSTRALIA
helenf.malone@bigpond.com
www.visualartist.info/helenmalone
0311, 0572, 0573

Kent Manske, USA
www.preneo.org
0300–0302

Marie Marcano, USA
marie.marcano@gmail.com
www.mariemarcano.com
0225, 0226, 0746, 0747

**Mary V. Marsh,
Quite Contrary Press**, USA
mvmarsh@earthlink.net
www.maryvmarsh.smugmug.com
0402

**Emily Martin,
Naughty Dog Press**, USA
emilyjmartin@mchsi.com
www.emilymartin.com
0549

Margaret Mason, AUSTRALIA
kozo63@wideband.net.au
0453

Anna Mavromatis, USA
annamavromatis@gmail.com
www.annamavromatis.com
0608, 0617, 0618

Lin Max, USA
lmax@sonic.net
www.lin-max.com
0289, 0290, 0566, 0567

Daniel Mayer, USA
daniel.mayer@asu.edu
http://soaportfolio.asu.edu/faculty/
mayer
0280, 0281

Mary Maynor, USA
mmaynor@swbell.net
www.marymaynor.com
0287, 0288, 0576

Mary McCarthy, USA
mccman@rcn.com
www.marymccarthybooks.com
0619, 0620

**Mary McCarthy and
Shirley Veenema**, USA
sveenema@verizon.net
0081

Sharon McCartney, USA
lilypeek@aol.com
www.sharonmccartneyart.com
0103–0105, 0947

**Alaska McFadden &
Jessica Elsaesser,
A Wrecked Tangle Press**, USA
awreckedtangle@gmail.com
www.awreckedtanglepress.com
0851, 0852, 0877, 0878

Lisa McGarry, ITALY
lisa@lisa-mcgarry.com
www.lisa-mcgarrycom
0559

Bhavna Mehta, Hansa Arts, USA
bhavnaumehta@gmail.com
www.bhavnamehta.com
0564, 0565

Fiona Merridew, USA
countmyfreckles@gmail.com
0451, 0452

**Barbara Milman,
Red Parrot Press**, USA
bam@barbaramilman.com
http://barbaramilman.com
0971

Richard Minsky, USA
www.minsky.com
0200–0202, 0335, 0999, 1000

**Lesley Mitchell,
Luminous Unit Press**, USA
lesley@lesleymitchell.com
www.lesleymitchell.com
0557, 0558, 0605, 0606

**Jeffrey Morin,
sailorBOYpress**, USA
jmorin@uwsp.edu
www.sailorboypress.com
0155, 0156

Bessie Smith Moulton, USA
besm@maine.rr.com
www.bessiesmithmoulton.
blogspot.com
0011, 0012, 0014, 0015, 0912, 0913

Amandine Nabarra-Piomelli, USA
amandine@anpfotos.com
www.anpfotos.com
0488, 0661, 0662

Irmari Nacht, USA
irmarinac@yahoo.com
www.irmari.com
0773, 0884, 0885

Catherine Nash, USA
cnash@wvcnet.com
www.catherinenash.com
0574, 0575, 0886, 0887, 0890, 0891

Bea Nettles, USA
nettles17@gmail.com
www.beanettles.com
0387, 0388, 0403, 0440

Sarah Nicholls, USA
sarah@sarahnicholls.com
www.sarahnicholls.com
0663–0665

Hanne Niederhausen, USA
niederhausen@netscape.net
www.niederhausen.net/hanne
0032, 0033, 0607

Carol Norby, USA
chnorby@citcom.net
www.carolhnorby.com
0991, 0992

**Bonnie Thompson Norman,
The Windowpane Press**, USA
inkdart@gmail.com
www.thewindowpanepress.com
0930, 0931

**Kelly O'Brien, TurningPointe
Press**, GERMANY
kelly@turningpointepress
www.turningpointepress.com
0110, 0111, 0771, 0772, 0783, 0784

Margy O'Brien, USA
margyobrien@gmail.com
www.margyobrien.com
0577

**Opie and Linda O'Brien, Burnt
Offerings Studio**, USA
gourdart@burntofferings.com
www.burntofferings.com
0376, 0383, 0384, 0393–0395

Bridget R. O'Donnell, USA
bodonne4@kent.edu
www.bridgetrodonnell.com
0468, 0469

Alis Olsen, USA
alisolsen@comcast.net
www.alisolsen.com
0286

Mo Orkiszewski, AUSTRALIA
mo@bluecatheaven.com.au
www.bluecatheaven.com.au
0267, 0268

**Adèle Outteridge,
Studio West End**, AUSTRALIA
delidge@uq.nef.au
www.studiowestend.com
0824, 0864, 0869, 0870

**Adèle Outteridge, Wim de Vos,
Studio West End**, AUSTRALIA
delidge@uq.nef.au
www.studiowestend.com
0867

Jan Owen, USA
janowenart@gmail.com
www.janowenart.com
0271–0273

Randi Parkhurst, USA
info@parkhurstpaperarts.com
www.parkhurstpaperarts.com
0757

Kelly Parsell, USA
parsellkelly@gmail.com
www.kellypaarsell.com
0316–0318

**Chad Pastotnik,
Deep Wood Press**, USA
chad@deepwoodpress.com
www.deepwoodpress.com
0086–0088

Pamela Paulsrud, USA
paulsrud@prodigy.net
wwwpamelapaulsrud.com
0755, 0756

Bettina Pauly, USA
bpaulysf@gmail.com
0428

Maureen Piggins, CANADA
maureen@maureenpiggins.com
www.maureenpiggins.com
0106, 0107

**Maria G. Pisano,
Memory Press**, USA
mgpstudio@aol.com
www.mariagpisano.com
0164, 0165, 0478

Sarah Plimpton, USA
sgp001@earthlink.net
www.ssarahplimpton.com
0681, 0682

Jill Pollock, USA
jpollock783@msn.com
0820, 0821

Susan Porteous, USA
sporteous@gmail.com
www.susanporteous.net
0707, 0708, 0818, 0819

Melissa Hilliard Potter, USA
potter.melissa@gmail.com
www.melissapotter.com
0312, 0313

Gail Prostrollo, USA
gail.prostrollo@gmail.com
www.gailprostrollo.net
0568, 0569

**Purgatory Pie Press, Dikko Faust
+ Esther K Smith, collaborating
artist: Michael Bartalos**, USA
esther@purgatorypiepress.com
www.purgatorypiepress.com
0933, 0934

**Purgatory Pie Press, Dikko Faust
+ Esther K Smith, collaborating
artist: Bill Fick**, USA
0609, 0610

**Purgatory Pie Press, Dikko Faust
+ Esther K Smith, collaborating
artist: Susan Happersett**, USA
0058, 0059

**Eleanore E. Ramsey,
Eleanore E. Ramsey Design
Bookbinding**, USA
eleanore.ramsey@sbcglobal.net
www.eleanoreramsey.com
0324, 0325, 0340, 0341

**Lisa Rappoport,
Littoral Press**, USA
cutvelvet@earthlink.net
www.littoralpress.com
0060–0062

Erica Spitzer Rasmussen, USA
erica.rasmussen@metrostate.edu
www.ericaspitzerrasmussen.com
0920–0922

**Felicia Rice,
Moving Parts Press**, USA
frice@movingpartspress.com
www.movingpartspress.com
0319, 0320

Benjamin D. Rinehart, USA
ben_rinehart@yahoo.com
www.benrinehart.com
0250, 0251, 0753, 0754

Camille Riner, USA
criner@dakotaphoto.com
0764

**Meda R. Rives, Veda M. Rives,
Mirror Image Press**, USA
info@mirrorimagepress.com
www.mirrorimagepress.com
0932

Josie Rodriguez, USA
josierod1@cox.net
www.josierodriguez.com
0733, 0734

Robert Roesch, USA
robert@robertroesch.com
www.robertroesch.com
0654, 0743–0745

**Bertha Rogers,
Six Swans Artist Editions**, USA
bkrogers@delhi.net
www.bertharogers.com
0022, 0023

Paulette Rosen, USA
pauletterosen@sbcglobal.net
0599, 0600

Evelyn Eller Rosenbaum, USA
evelyn@evelyneller.com
www.evelyneller.com
0421, 0422

Maddy Rosenberg, USA
maddrose@gmail.com
www.maddyrosenberg.net
0385, 0386, 0417, 0418

Marilyn R. Rosenberg, USA
bmrosenberg@netscape.net
www.peekskillartists.org/node/48
0822, 0944, 0945

Pien Rotterdam, Water Leaf Press,
THE NETHERLANDS
pien.rotterdam@home.nl
www.waterleafpaperandwords.
com
0528–0530

**Sibyl Rubottom,
Bay Park Press**, USA
sibyl.rubottom@att.net
www.bayparkpress.com
0255–0257, 0506

**Jamie Runnells,
Jamie Runnells Designs**, USA
jrunnells@caad.msstate.edu
www.jamierunnells.com
0856, 0857

**Laura Russell,
Simply Books, Ltd.**, USA
simplybooksltd@gmail.com
www.laurarussell.net
0364, 0370–0372

Regula Russelle, USA
regula@cedarfencepress.com
www.cedarfencepress.com
0823, 0973

Cathy Ryan, USA
cathy_ryan@mac.com
0464, 0465, 0497, 0498

**Linda Samson-Talleur, La
Ginestra**, USA
ltalleur@ku.edu
0365, 0366

Helen Sanderson, AUSTRALIA
helen@helensanderson.com.au
www.helensanderson.com.au
0459, 0915

Rocco Scary, USA
roc.scary@verizon.net
www.roccoscary.com
0082, 0083, 0647, 0648

Miriam Schaer, USA
mschaer@earthlink.net
http://miriamschaer.com
0917, 0918

Ashley L. Schick, USA
ashleylschick@gmail.com
www.ashleylschick.com
0434, 0435

Brooke Schmidt, USA
flypeterfly@hotmail.com
www.brookeschmidt.etsy.com
0834, 0835

**Judith Serebrin, Judith of Serebrin
Books & Prints**, USA
serebrin@sbcglobal.net
0024–0026, 0656, 0659, 0660

C J. Shane, USA
shane@cjshane.com
www.cjshane.com
0159, 0160, 0359

**Sharon A. Sharp,
Sharp Handmade Books/
Curious Pursuits Press**, USA
sharon@sharphandmadebooks.
com
www.sharphandmadebooks.com
0224

**Carolyn Shattuck, Shattuck
Studio & Gallery**, USA
shattuck@sover.net
www.shattuckgallery.com
0993

Elizabeth Beronich Sheets, USA
lizartseattle@gmail.com
www.facebook.com/Elizabeth-
BeronichSheets
0410–0415

Ellen Sheffield, Unit IV Arts, USA
sheffiel@kenyon.edu
www.ellensheffield.com
0461, 0462, 0470–0472

Genie Shenk, USA
agshenk@match.ucsd.edu
0020, 0021, 0042, 0043, 0914

**C.B. Sherlock,
Seymour Press**, USA
cbsherlock@yahoo.com
www.cbsherlock.com
0621

Stephanie Sherwood, USA
ssherwood@insight.rr.com
0044, 0045

Elena Mary Siff, USA
esiff@att.net
www.elenamarysiff.com
0630, 0631

**Robbin Ami Silverberg,
Dobbin Mill/Dobbin Books**, USA
dobbinmill@earthlink.net
www.robbinamisilverberg.com
0064–0069, 0840, 0841

Jana Sim, USA
jana@janasim.com
www.janasim.com
0093, 0094, 0438, 0685–0687

Barbara Simler, CANADA
moonandhare@gmail.com
http://barbarasimler.com
0019, 0314, 0315

Shawn Kathleen Simmons, USA
shawnksimmons@gmail.com
www.shawnksimmons.com
0811, 0812

Alice Simpson, USA
alice@alicesimpson.com
www.alicesimpson.com
0362, 0363

Lynn Skordal, USA
generalone@comcast.net
www.lynnskordal.paspartout.com
0584–0586, 0589, 0590

Dolph Smith, USA
dolph@tennarkippi.com
0354, 0748–0751

Vicki Smith, USA
vicki-smith.art@gmail.com
www.vickismithart.com
0612

Jan Sobota, CZECH REPUBLIC
jan@jsobota.cz
www.jsobota.cz
0326, 0737, 0738

Jarmila Jelena Sobotova,
CZECH REPUBLIC
jarmila.sobota@gmail.com
www.jsobota.cz
0865, 0866, 0916

Buzz Spector, USA
spector@samfox.wustl.edu
www.buzzspector.com
0115, 0116

**Laurie Spitz, Amee Pollack,
Spitz & Pollack**, USA
spitzandpollack@yahoo.com
www.ameejpollack.com
0715–0718

**Jessica Spring,
Springtide Press**, USA
springtidepress@me,com
www.springtidepresscom
0456, 0457, 0994, 0995

Marilyn Stablein, USA
marilynstablein@msn.com
0611

Alice Stanne, USA
alicestanne@gmail.com
www.alicestanne.com
0444

Kevin Steele, USA
MrKevinSteele@hotmail.com
www.mrkevinsteele.com
0615, 0616

**Gail Stiffe,
Hands on Paper**, AUSTRALIA
gail_stiffe@yahoo.com
www.gailstiffe.info
0344, 0345, 0888, 0889

Cindy Stiteler, USA
cinderup@gmail.com
0282, 0283

Judith E. Strom, USA
quarksmom@jeffbb.net
0284, 0285

Kathy Strother, USA
bookartist@bellsouth.net
0441, 0442

Margaret Suchland, USA
margaretsuchland@me.com
www.margaretsuchland.com
0429, 0430, 0460

Lynn Sures, USA
lynn@lynnsures.com
www.lynnsures.com
0800, 0980

**Erin Sweeney, Lovely In
The Home Press**, USA
erin@erinsweeney.net
www.erinsweeny.net
0027–0029, 0091, 0092, 0787, 0909

Earle D. Swope, USA
earleswope@gmail.com
wwwearleswope.com
0942, 0943

Eriko Takahashi, USA
etet.arts@gmail.com
0458, 0552, 0553

Mary Tasillo,
Citizen Hydra Projects, USA
mary@citizenhydra.net
www.citizenhydra.net
0258, 0259, 0593–0595

Jen Thomas, Veronica Press, USA
jen_thomas@mac.com
www.flickr.com/photos/jenthomas
0580, 0581, 0792–0794

Peter & Donna Thomas, USA
peteranddonna@cruzio.com
0063, 0078–0080, 0637, 0677, 0678,
0690, 0691

Andie Thrams, USA
andiethrams@earthlink.net
www.andiethrams.com
0613, 0614

Jill Timm,
Mystical Places Press, USA
jtimm@aol.com
www.mysticalplaces.com
0439, 0596

Eugenie Torgerson, USA
eugenietorgerson@sbcglobal.net
http://blog.eugenietorgerson.com
0752, 0801, 0802

Richard Troncone, USA
richtroncone@yahoo.com
www.richtroncone.com
0297, 0298

Rae Trujillo, Raes of Sun, USA
lazlo.trujillo@comcast.net
www.raesofsun.com
0263, 0264

Juanita H. Tumelaire,
Impmaker Press, USA
impmaker@comcast.net
www.impmaker.com
0499, 0500

Terence Uren, AUSTRALIA
terence.uren@bigpond.com
www.canberrabookbinders.org.au
0274

Edward van Vliet, CANADA
etechne@yahooca
www.edwardvanvliet.ca; www.
etechne.blogspot.ca
0739–0741

Merike van Zanten,
Double Dutch Design, USA
merike@earthlink.net
www.doubledutch-design.com
0832, 0833, 0905, 0906

Kestutis Vasiliunas, LITHUANIA
kestutis@vasiliunas.arts.lt
http://vasiliunas.arts.lt/
http://vasiliunas.artistsbook.lt/
0561–0563, 0967

Tom Virgin, USA
tom@tomvirgin.com
www.tomvirgin.com
0897, 0898, 0950–0952

Sarah Vogel, Slow Industries, USA
sfeeneyvogel@gmail.com
www.slowindustries.wordpress.
com
0554, 0555

Stefan Volatile-Wood, USA
stefan.volatilewood@gmail.com
http://stefanvolatilewood.tumblr.
com
0054, 0055

Nancy Jean Wallace,
Too Many Shoes Studio, USA
toomanyshoes2@comcast.net
0013

Robert Walp,
Chester Creek Press, USA
bob@chestercreekpress.com
www.chestercreekpress.com
0342, 0343

Shu-Ju Wang, USA
shuju@fivebats.com
www.fingerstothebone.com
0826, 0827

Patricia Sarrafian Ward, USA
pishaward@gmail.com
www.patriciasarrafianward.com
0131, 0132, 0432, 0433

Marama Warren,
The Creative Spirit, AUSTRALIA
marama@internode.on.net
0379

Fran Watson, USA
fwwatson@san.rr.com
www.franwatsonart.com
0495

Sandy Webster, USA
wstudio55@hotmail.com
www.sandywebster.com
0578, 0579, 0736, 0883

Beata Wehr, USA
beatawehr@gmail.com
www.beatawehr.com
0056, 0057, 0278, 0279, 0350, 0351

Anastasia Weigle,
"In a Bind" Studio, USA
anastasia.weigle@gmail.com
www.anastasiaweigle.artspan.com
0622, 0623

Suzanne Lydia Weinert, USA
suzannelydia@hotmail.com
www.bookearrings.com
0548, 0628, 0629

Marcia Weisbrot,
Pencilhead Press, USA
marcia@marciaweisbrot.com
www.marciawisbrot.com
0806, 0807

Stephanie Wilde,
Smith and Wilde Press, USA
stephaniew@stewartgallery.com
http://stephaniewildeart.com
0632, 0633

Jody Williams,
Flying Paper Press, USA
jody_williams@mcad.edu
www.flyingpaperpress.com
0157, 0158, 0169, 0170, 0923, 0924

Thomas Parker Williams, USA
tpwilliams89@gmail.com
www.thomasparkerwilliams.com
0126, 0127, 0137, 0138, 0962–0964

Beverly Ann Wilson, USA
corvuscodex@gmail.com
www.corvuscodex.com
0242, 0591, 0592

Michelle Wilson,
Rocinante Press, USA
rocinantepress@gmail.com
www.michellewilsonprojects.com
0049–0051, 0360, 0361

Maria Winkler, USA
mpwinkler@yahoo.com
www.mariawinkler.com
0624, 0625

Sandra Winkworth, AUSTRALIA
swinkie@bigpond.com
0582, 0583

Rutherford Witthus,
φ **(Phi Press)**, USA
rutherford.witthus@gmail.com
www.rutherfordwitthus.com
0275, 0276

Jacqueline L. Wygant,
One O.A.K. Book Arts, USA
oneoakbookarts@gmail.com
www.oneoakbookarts.blogspot.
com
0670, 0671

Nanette Wylde,
Hunger Rotten Books, USA
nanette@hungerbutton.org
www.hungerbutton.org
0239–0241

Irina Yablochkina, RUSSIA
iablotchki@yandex.ru
www.iablochki.narod.ru
0761–0763

Dennis Yuen, USA
me@dennisyuen.com
www.dennisyuenCom
0277, 0293, 0815, 0816

Philip Zimmermann, USA
pzim@spaceheat.com
www.spaceheat.com;
www.philipzimmermann.
blogspot.com
0260–0262

[Acknowledgements

We want to thank the very creative people at Quarry Books. This book would not have happened without the vision of, and clear direction from acquisitions editor Mary Ann Hall and publisher Winnie Prentiss. We have valued and appreciated the good spirits and competence of the whole Quarry team for this book, which included Cora, Tiffany, and David. They have made our job as authors seem easy.

Thanks must also be given to the artists featured within these pages. Their endless and exciting exploration of all facets of book creation is inspiring. We admire their real appreciation of each other's work and their generous spirit of giving credit where credit is due, whether it's the development of a new book structure or binding technique or use of an unexpected medium.

Many of the artists included in this book teach classes on various aspects of the book arts all over the world. If you find yourself inspired to learn more, please check the Internet for websites of artists that you find most inspiring to see if they'll be holding a workshop near you or look for courses and workshops at book arts centers, at college, university, and trade schools, paper and materials retailers, or adult community extension schools in your region. The dialog on "what is an artists' book?" will continue for many years, and there's room more voices. It's an inclusive, enthusiastic conversation: join in!

[About the Authors

SANDRA SALAMONY is the author of *1,000 Jewelry Inspirations* and co-author of *1,000 Artisan Textiles* and *1,000 Ideas for Decorating Cupcakes, Cookies & Cakes*. In addition, she was the graphic designer for other books in Quarry's 1,000 series, all of which resulted in Mark Lipinski of Creative Mojo naming her "the queen of 1,000 everything."

Sandra has been involved in the business of creating books for many years: studying publication design at the New England School of Art and Design, working as creative director at Sky Publishing, and now running a business as a freelance book and magazine designer. But it all began at age 9 with a dos-à-dos drum leaf-bound book of original text and hand-drawn graphite illustrations that she created with her sister Gina, containing a catalog of their possessions that they were willing to sell to their friends.

PETER AND DONNA THOMAS, authors and illustrators of *More Making Books by Hand: Exploring Miniature Books, Alternative Structures, and Found Objects* (Quarry Books, 2004) are self-employed book artists, papermakers, and letterpress printers who write, illustrate, and bind their own books. They have been making books for over 30 years, having learned to print from William Everson, using a Washington hand press. In the 1970s, as craftspeople at the Renaissance Pleasure Faire, they fell in love with gypsy wagons and built one to use for selling their wares. In 2010–2012, as wandering book artists, they took their gypsy wagon on a 235 day tour, through 35 states, teaching book arts classes, giving lectures, blogging, seeing the sights, and generally assessing the state of the book arts in the USA as they worked on this book.

Peter & Donna Thomas